D1536478

The
Music
Internet
Untangled

Using Online Services to
Expand Your Musical Horizons

Andy Breeding

Published in October 2004 by

Giant Path Publishing
148 Standish Road
Watertown, MA 02472
617-972-1708

Find us on the World Wide Web at http://www.giantpath.com. To report errors or make comments and suggestions, please send a note to feedback@giantpath.com.

© 2004 by Giant Path Publishing.   All Rights Reserved.

Notice of Rights

All rights reserved. No part of this book may be reproduced, stored in a retrieval system, or transmitted in any form or by any means, electronic, mechanical, recording or otherwise, without the prior permission of Giant Path Publishing.

Notice of Liability

The information in this book is distributed on an "As Is" basis, without warranty. While every precaution has been taken in the preparation of the book, neither the author nor Giant Path Publishing shall have any liability to any person or entity with respect to any loss or damage caused or alleged to be caused directly or indirectly by the information contained in this book or by the computer software and Internet services described in it.

Trademarks

Throughout this book, trademarks are used. Rather than put a trademark symbol in every occurrence of a trademarked name, we state that we are using the names in an editorial fashion only with no intention of infringement of the trademark.

ISBN: 1-932340-02-5

Publishers Cataloging-In-Publication Data

Breeding, Andy, 1962-
    The music internet untangled: using online services to expand your musical
    horizons/by Andy Breeding.
        p. cm.
    Includes index.
    ISBN 1-932340-02-5 (pbk.)
    1. Music—Computer network resources. 2. Music—Computer programs.
    3. Internet—Computer programs. I. Title.
ML74.7 .B74 2004
025.06'78—dc21

Produced in the United States of America

005.7
B83

SYS 3697325
9-05

Table of Contents

Preface

As a teenager, music was really important to me. It was my refuge—a huge and multicolored world of rebellion, sexuality, and spiritual and political transformation. From the safety of my bedroom, I experienced the greatness that was Rock in the 1970s. I took pride in my knowledge of popular music that mattered. This era, and the sense of wonder and discovery that I felt while listening to this music, were perfectly captured in the coming-of-age movie, *Almost Famous* (2000).

As I got older, I devoted less time to musical interests. I got married, started my career, and generally got busier. Thanks to college radio and some good local acts, I did keep in touch with some exciting new music—but in general I became more disconnected from the music scene, feeling my age as I failed to recognize the new music that streamed out at me from radios, movies and public places. As a teenager I was a music snob, taking pity on lesser mortals who filled their lives with the shallow, inferior pop music being hawked by the media conglomerates. But one day I woke up and realized that I was out of touch, that my former position as savvy music lover had given way to nostalgia and "classic rock" radio on the way to work. Looking back, I pretty much slept though the emergence of Rap, Hip Hop, and Electronica. A whole new generation of performers was unknown to me. By the time I heard about Napster, and understood what it could do, it was in the process of being shut down.

So what was I to do? I disliked much of the new music I was hearing on the radio. When I did go to the record store I was confronted with a huge body of music I knew little about. In-store music merchandising had become slicker, making me feel less at home. I even had trouble figuring out which categories a lot of music belonged in (and I was a professional librarian!). Wading through the bins was not working for me.

Then one day at work a friend told me about a new Internet service called LAUNCHcast—which allows users to rate music and receive a personalized music stream based on their preferences. This music experience went far beyond the boundaries of what I was used to on commercial radio. LAUNCHcast allowed me to subscribe to other listener's "stations" if I liked their taste. It was free and smart, and most importantly it put me in the driver's seat.

I could enjoy it right at work, thanks to my company's broadband connection. No muss, no fuss. No schlepping to the record store. Here I could make my comeback to informed fandom from the comfort and privacy of my own cube.

Thus began my realization that the Internet could help me get back in the game. Although I didn't have the time and energy to pursue new music as I did as a teenager, the new tools made it so much easier to discover and listen to good new music—that I could cover more ground than I ever did before. Hallelujah!

As a corporate librarian, well versed in the power of online databases and search engines, I knew how to assess online tools and make them serve my needs. As new Internet-based services came online, I found more ways to turbo-charge my music discovery process. Contrary to what I thought before—there are lots of good recordings being released. Beyond the wasteland of commercial radio and mass marketed "star" artists lie rich fields of vital, vibrant music—largely invisible to the masses—but easily found if you have the right tools.

As I started doing research for this book, and began using more of the new Internet music services, something else dawned on me. Huge libraries of music were suddenly available to me—collections that dwarfed the best record collections of my dreams. I began exploring music in ways that I never had before. Then it became clear to me. A new era for music fans has begun.

Acknowledgments

I'd like to thank the people who reviewed the manuscript and provided helpful suggestions and feedback: Rick Lugg, Harlen Welsh, Scott McGrath, Renee Moelders, and Jeff Hamill. Thanks also to my wife Anne, whose support and feedback has been crucial in moving this project forward.

Introduction

Now is a time of unprecedented change and opportunity for music lovers everywhere. Amid the turbulence of industry upheaval, a new generation of online music services is emerging to transform the way we access, use, and pay for recorded music. We are entering a new era of musical abundance.

No longer are our listening choices dictated by the contents of our CD collection or the content of our local airwaves. With an Internet connection, we can expand our home music library a hundredfold for less than the cost of one CD per month—legally! We can transcend the limitations of local radio and listen to broadcasts from around the globe. A new world of listening options is just a mouse click away.

Discover New Music

What's more, online music services make the process of exploring the world of music dramatically easier, making it possible for time-starved people to experience a new world of music enjoyment. With over 38,000 full-length recordings released each year in the United States alone, the task of finding the best music is harder than ever. Somewhere out there is music that will make a difference in your life, and do more of what you want it to do—whether you are looking to be energized or sedated, comforted or challenged, inspired or consoled. Using powerful new tools you can navigate the huge world of recorded music—once a daunting task—and find new music to fit your tastes and desires. No longer does it require large amounts of time and commitment to seek out and find the best in modern music, or to become knowledgeable about today's music genres, artists, and recordings. All it takes is a computer and an Internet connection.

Step into the Driver's Seat

Once you find music you enjoy, you can take control and customize your listening experience in ways that simply weren't possible in the past. New tools allow you to create personalized radio broadcasts, filter music according to your taste and moods, and create personal music mixes for any occasion. New ways to buy music provide you with more control over how and when you pay for your music. For instance, it is now possible to buy access to music for a limited period of time, or to buy individual songs rather than an entire album. It is possible to pay one price for the ability to play a song online, and another price for the ability to play the song online and copy the song to a CD or portable music player. Perhaps most exciting of all is the emergence of "all you can drink" subscription plans, which provide access to huge libraries of music for a flat monthly payment.

What's more, using these services can free you from dependence on music industry promotional practices that favor a handful of star acts packaged for mass consumption. It is now easier to seek out and find quality, independent music—music that was practically invisible in the past. If you believe that today's music scene has little to offer you, think again. There's lots of great music out there, and thanks to online music services, it's now easy to find and enjoy.

The Road to Musical Riches

This book provides you with a tour of the different kinds of Internet-based music services, and shows you how to use them to increase your listening enjoyment. You'll learn what each kind of service has to offer and come away with the knowledge to pick the services that are right for you. I have highlighted and discussed the services that I believe are most worthy of attention.

Once you've learned about the different ways to access music online, you'll move into the rich world of music information, where you'll learn how to navigate the ocean of available music, and to find and select music that matters to you. In the process, you will learn how to become more knowledgeable about music. You will learn how to quickly:

- Find reviews for a given recording
- Use awards and "best-of" lists to identify critically praised recordings
- Get educated about new genres of music
- Identify important artists and albums for each genre
- Find detailed artist information, song lyrics, and chart information

The music discovery plans presented in Part Three will give you the means to convert your new understanding into action. Structured, seven-day programs are provided to help you get up-to-speed with the highlighted services.

So Why Pay?

With music available on the file-trading networks for free, you might ask this. Many of the services highlighted in this book ask you to open your wallet in exchange for what they have to offer. The reasons are many. First, the best of these services provide a better experience for the consumer. Getting music is quicker and easier, and you have the assurance that the music you ask for is what you're going to be getting—free of viruses, annoying pop-up ads, and spyware that invades your privacy. They save the busy person's time.

Discovering good, new music is also much easier using these services, with their rich music information and exploration capabilities. Second, by paying for access to music you ensure that artists get paid for their work. If you value music and the contribution that artists make to our culture, then you'll agree it's worth compensating them for it. Last, you avoid the legal risks involved in using the file-trading networks. In recent months, the music industry has successfully sued people for using these networks to violate copyright law.

When you see what the best services can do, you'll agree: they're worth it!

The Dawn of a New Era?

Until recently, most press coverage of online music has focused on the controversies surrounding file sharing and music piracy. Scarcely a week went by without some dire pronouncement coming from one side or the other in the copyright wars. The music industry, on the one hand, claimed to be protecting its very existence from pirates and consumers eager to avoid paying for music. Copyright activists and music fans, on the other hand, opposed what they saw as corporate attempts to protect inflated prices and criminalize legitimate uses of purchased music. Belated and lackluster attempts by record companies to provide online music services were met with derision by fans and critics alike, many of whom resented music industry attempts to block access to free file sharing services like Napster.

In this atmosphere of negativity, it was hard to find journalists writing anything that was positive about online music, even though good services were available. With the success of Apple's iTunes Music Store, and the launch of similar downloading services, the tone has changed. The journalistic chorus tells us that the record companies finally "get it," and that music fans are advised to try the new services. What they aren't telling us, is that there is a world of online music beyond downloading, and that it is well worth exploring.

Being Current

As the shift to online music picks up speed over the next few years, the changes will come rapidly. To keep pace, this book will be updated twice per year. More frequent updates will be made available via the Giantpath.com Web site. While some content in this book will go out-of-date—such as prices and service specifics—the principles required to understand online music services and get the most out of them will not. Subsequent editions will include coverage of new services and features and as well as revised recommendations and discussion of significant changes to existing services.

A Few Caveats

Although the file-trading services are quite popular and do have legitimate uses—including some fee-based services that have recently become available—I will not be discussing them at any great length in this book. The focus here is on legitimate music services that respect copyright law and see to it that artists and copyright holders are paid for their work. Also, this book does not focus on the technologies that are used to deliver these services. Its primary focus is on why these services are important and how to get the most out of them. New terms and concepts will be explained as necessary, but detailed technical explanations are left to other books.

Part One

Internet Music Services

Internet Radio
Leaving Your Home Town

Internet radio is the best place to start when seeking out new music on the Internet. It's the simplest type of online music service to use. It's cheap, and offers riches that cannot be found elsewhere.

Remember When You First Got Cable TV?

I remember when our family first got cable TV and went from having a handful of TV channels to what seemed like a huge number—perhaps thirty stations. My jaw dropped when I saw all those stations. In an instant, the landscape changed. It's the same with Internet radio, except with Internet radio you aren't limited to the offerings of one or perhaps two providers, as you are with cable TV. Internet radio providers number in the thousands, ranging from large media corporations to artists promoting their work to teenagers operating out of their bedrooms. No longer are you limited to the local airwaves.

You can now tune in to the offerings of broadcasters across the country and around the world. For Jamaican music you can now go right to Jamaica; for the latest in British pop, right to England. Interested in surf music? The best surf music station I know of comes from Buck's County, Pennsylvania.

Hot and Cold Running Music

While many Internet radio stations are traditional radio stations that have made their broadcasts Internet accessible, others were created as Internet-only stations. Some of these resemble traditional stations and run different programs in different time slots. Many others, however, focus on one particular musical theme or style, providing 24 x 7 access to that music—a musical faucet of sorts, a single program. Turn it on and music will be playing. You won't hear news on the hour, DJ chatter, or traffic reports. If you tire of listening to one station, or if a different mood overtakes you, a multitude of stations are a mouse click away. Inexpensive to operate, these single-focus stations represent an important new option for music lovers. They allow listeners to dial up musical styles and themes with a specificity and ease that didn't exist before. Provided you know where to look, an astonishing variety of musical styles can be found. These include focused genres like doo-wop, flamenco, or death metal; music from specific periods like the "roaring 20s"; or a combination of both, such as 70s English progressive rock. Other stations address a theme (e.g., holiday music, love songs) or an activity (e.g., workout music, wedding music). Looking for the sound of a particular instrument, such as bagpipes or the banjo? There are stations devoted to them. For chart watchers, there are stations whose playlists countdown the music rankings. Other stations, like Rhapsody's "Best of 2003" station, only play music from "best-of" lists. Of course, there are also large numbers of conventional stations which play main-stream, commercial music as well.

Internet Radio Tells You What You Are Listening To

Knowing what you are listening to is central to music discovery. Internet radio can make this easy by supplying song and artist information with each song as it is played. This information appears on the media player display on your computer. From here, many services provide links allowing you to access more information about the recording: purchasing information, record reviews, and artist biographies. These services are information rich.

It's Cheaper Than Buying CDs

In the past if you wanted to hear a specific kind of music—Gregorian chant for example—you needed to play a CD or record that you owned. There was no radio station that provided that kind of music, reliably, 24 hours a day. Now you can fill this need with Internet radio and have no need to buy a recording. So long as you don't require absolute control over which music gets played, and in which order it gets played, then a targeted radio station will fill the need. Most Internet radio stations cost nothing to access beyond the cost of your Internet connection. Others are available by subscription, as fee-based, "premium" offerings.

Ads Can be Avoided, for a Price

Typically, premium stations will offer ad-free programming and high-quality audio streams. Unlike with traditional broadcast radio, access to Internet radio can be restricted to paying subscribers, in the same way that access to cable TV can. This enables fee-based stations to provide ad-free listening alternatives. If advertisements annoy you, you can now get rid of them, for a price. As of this writing, $5 per month (or less if you pay yearly) is a common price for access to a collection of premium, ad-free radio stations.

What You Need to Get Started

To access Internet radio and other Internet music services you need a personal computer, a sound card (most PCs have one), and speakers. You'll also need an Internet connection, preferably a high speed one (cable modem, DSL, or ISDN).

Media player software is also required to play music streams that are broadcast by Internet radio stations. More than likely you already have such software installed on your computer. If not, it can be freely available obtained and downloaded via the Internet. Because there is more than one flavor of Internet broadcast (think AM vs. FM), you'll need more than one player to be able to listen to all the available stations. Most Internet radio station Web sites provide links to Web pages where you can obtain the necessary player software required to listen to their broadcasts. To start exploring Internet radio you can take one of two options:

1. Use the media player that came with your computer
The easiest way to sample Internet radio is to use the media player that comes bundled with your computer or computer operating system. For Windows PC users this means *Windows Media Player*. For Apple Macintosh users this means the *iTunes* player. Each of these players has a "radio tuner" which provides access to hundreds of free radio stations.

2. Sign up for an Internet radio service
Sign up for one of the radio services recommended in this book. Many are free. Those that aren't offer free trials. The services I recommend include Live365, MSN Radio, LAUNCHcast, and Musicmatch Radio. Each of these services has a chapter devoted to it—to help you decide. Once you've read up on one of these services and decided you'd like to try it, go to Part Three, *Internet Music Discovery Plans*, where you'll find a concrete seven-day plan for getting up to speed with that service.

Internet radio services are fewer in number than individual stations but provide the easiest, most productive way to get started with Internet radio. I define an Internet radio service as a collection of radio stations offered through a single organization, and accessible from a single dedicated player interface. The player is customized to provide links to music information, interactive features, and personalization options. These services make the world of Internet radio more manageable by providing a limited number of station choices, and providing richer and more consistent information about the stations that are available. In some cases, they also help the music explorer by providing rich access to artist and album information, as well as providing tools for people to find music that they like.

Individual radio stations can be located using Internet radio directories, Web directories such as Yahoo, and search engines such as Google.

MAJOR INTERNET RADIO DIRECTORIES AND TUNERS

RealGuide Radio Tuner - http://realguide.real.com/tuner
For users of RealPlayer software: a directory of over 3,200 radio stations broadcasting RealAudio streams, searchable by genre, band (AM, FM or Internet Only), language, and location. Stations can be browsed by broad genre category. Listings include premium radio stations.

Windows Radio Tuner - http://www.windowsmedia.com/radiotuner
For users of Microsoft's Windows Media Player: a directory of radio stations broadcasting in the Windows Media format. Comparable to the RealGuide tuner but adds the ability to search stations by their streaming bit rate (e.g., 56K, T1).

SHOUTcast Directory - http://shoutcast.com
3,500+ stations broadcasting MP3 streams using the SHOUTcast freeware streaming audio software. Features not found in the Real or Microsoft directories include usage based popularity figures, a more detailed genre classification scheme, and in many cases a display of the track that a station is currently playing.

iTunes Radio Tuner
Computers with the *iTunes* music player/jukebox software have access to the iTunes radio directory—which lists MP3 streams that can be played by *iTunes*. The current version contains approximately 300 stations and is browseable by genre. Not available on the Web.

Live365 Directory - http://www.live365.com/index.live
A directory of radio stations that broadcast MP3 and MP3PRO streams via the Live365 broadcasting service. As big as any of the others, but with richer search options. All stations are accessible using Live365's dedicated player.

Yahoo and Google Directory Listings
Listings include radio stations and radio services/networks. Inclusion here is an indicator of relative size and popularity.

Yahoo: http://dir.yahoo.com/Entertainment/Music/Internet_Broadcasts
Google: http://directory.google.com/Top/Arts/Radio/Internet

Using Internet Radio

Listening to radio is more convenient than playing your own music. You don't have to select the recording or worry about which songs to play next. Someone else takes care of this. What's more, you are exposed to new music that you've never heard before. You never know what's going to be played next. This keeps things interesting. Add the tremendous new variety and functionality that Internet radio provides, and new possibilities open up.

Taking advantage of these possibilities requires some action on our part, some new listening strategies. Let's consider the fact that you now have access to *thousands* of stations. Such a wealth of stations invites greater exploration, and requires a greater taste for adventure if you are to claim the treasure that is out there. Living by the ocean is different than living on a pond. You can venture out in a number of ways:

- **Listen to genre-specific stations for new types of music**
  Rather than focus exclusively on music genres that you know and like, take the time to listen to music that is new or unfamiliar. This includes music that was popular in previous eras. Pick a genre or style and give it some time to work its particular magic. Think about how it makes you feel, and remember that you can recreate that feeling by tuning back in. Using this approach, I have come to like such forms as dub, surf music, and movie soundtracks from the 60s and 70s.

- **Sample the music of a particular country, region, or culture**
  Perhaps you are going on a trip soon or wonder what people in other countries are listening to. Using radio station directories, you can easily find stations broadcasting from a country or city of interest. Alternately you can find single focus stations devoted to music from a particular region or culture (e.g., Hawaiian music, African soukous music, Japanese pop, bagpipe music). Be a world traveler.

- **Experiment with music you can listen to while working**
  Though purists might wish it otherwise, the fact is that we inhabit a world of multi-tasking, where we listen to music while doing something else: driving, doing chores, working. While rote tasks can be accompanied by most any music, tasks requiring conscious thought and attention are best accompanied by less obtrusive music, music that is less demanding of our attention. This music works at the peripheries, establishing a mood or a feeling. Options here extend beyond traditional "easy listening" music to include stations that play ambient music, downtempo electronica, New Age music, and certain types of classical and instrumental music.

- **Use specific stations to modulate your energy level or mood**
  Researchers studying people in commercial environments have long known that music can be used in a functional way to facilitate or reinforce certain moods or mental states. By tuning in to certain Internet radio stations, you can use it this way also. For example, when my mind is getting too busy and I need to calm down, I listen to a station called Astreaux World (http://www.live365.com/stations/astreaux), which plays "ambient, New Age, space music" that is meditative in quality. If I need to bring things up a notch I'll switch to EMjoy, a downtempo electronica station (http://www.live365.com/stations/fkorf) that is also relaxing, if a bit livelier. After lunch, if I'm starting to sag, I might switch to Devlar Surf Sessions, a surf music station (http://www.live365.com/stations/surfinstro) which plays upbeat, instrumental music that I find energizing.

- **Troll for the bizarre, the unusual, and the novel**
  Looking for something different? Live365, a service profiled in the next chapter, has stations devoted to: Disney Resort music, music from the TV show "The Sopranos", anime movie soundtracks, video game music, World War II radio programs, Philadelphia Mummers music, Renaissance fair music, belly dancing music, sea shanties, and more!

What's Wrong with Traditional Radio?

Many people are dissatisfied with the state of commercial radio in the U.S. today. "It all sounds the same" and "there's nothing there for me" are common complaints. Observers point to consolidation in the radio industry as the cause. Since 1996, when Congress deregulated the radio industry, a wave of mergers has placed the majority of radio stations into the hands of a few large corporations. During this time the number of independent radio stations shrank. Uniform corporate policies and market research-driven programming have reduced the variety of music on commercial radio. One critic summed up this approach as "play the fewest songs that appeal to the most people." Also problematic is the requirement that record companies make big payments to promoters in order to get their songs on the radio. As a consequence it is harder than ever for new acts to be heard on commercial radio; only the biggest and best-financed acts get access to the commercial airwaves. Bill Wyman of the Rolling Stones recently said, "The Rolling Stones would never make it now."

Narrowing Down Your Choices

Of course having access to thousands of stations presents its own problems. How to narrow down the choices? One way is to subscribe to an Internet radio service and use its stations exclusively. Each service aims to provide a radio universe of sorts, though some have more variety than others. Decide on which genres are critical for you, and how much variety and eclecticism you desire. Then look at the available services.

Other factors to consider:

- **How good is the dedicated player and interface?**
  Is it easy to use, with rich information and customization options? Will it run on your computer?

- **Does the service have an ad-free offering?**
  Are you willing to pay to get ad-free programming?

- **What audio quality or streaming bit rate do you prefer?**
  You may be an audiophile who requires the highest possible bit rate and audio quality for your streams. Alternately you might have a dial-up connection and be limited to smaller bit rate streams.

- **Is it important to you to hear the voice of a disc jockey (DJ)?**
  By and large, stations on Internet radio services do not have a DJ on hand to talk to you between the songs. They tend to be pre-programmed and display the playlist information in the radio player. For a DJ's voice (recorded or live) you'll need to seek out traditional radio stations that simulcast on the Internet or one of the few Internet-only radio stations that feature live DJs.

The next two chapters discuss two Internet radio services that I recommend: Live365 and MSN Radio.

> "I use music as fuel. If I need to get into a certain mindset I know there's certain songs that I can turn on that just—that's the gas! And that'll get me right where I need to go. Or if I need to get out of a certain state, I'll put on this song or that song—and it just propels you."
>
> - John Cusack (Interview from DVD version of the movie *High Fidelity*)

2

Live365: The Place to Start

Live365 is an excellent place to explore the richness of Internet radio. This service provides access to over 5,000 radio stations playing just about every conceivable kind of music. What differentiates Live365 from other Internet radio services is not only the depth of its offerings, but also the ability of its directory and search engine to help you find stations of interest.

Also unique is Live365's role as incubator of the "radio revolution." Live365 provides tools for individuals and business to create Internet radio stations, which are then hosted on Live365 servers and publicized through Live365's directory. In addition, Live365 has used its home page to encourage listeners to get involved in public policy issues that affect the fledging Internet radio industry. With over three million listeners per month, they are a major force in Internet radio.

With Live365, you can browse stations in approximately 60 genre categories or search for stations using a range of search criteria, including:

- **Keywords** – Used by broadcasters to describe their station.

- **Artist / CD / track names** – Allows you to search station playlists.

- **Station category** – Is it professional or amateur? Is it broadcast live?

- **Editor's picks** – Have Live365 editors highlighted the station?

Station listings provide other useful information including TOTAL LISTENER HOURS, which tell you how much a station has been listened to in the last 30 days; STATION RATINGS, which tells you how the listeners have rated the station; and SPEED, which tells you the bit rate (sound quality) that a station is streaming at.

Music Discovery with Live365

Think of Live365 as a giant library of on-demand musical styles and program-ming mixes. Or a portal into the record collections of music aficionados the world over. The sheer scope and range of offerings promote serendipity—the accidental discoveries of new music you would never have thought to seek out. Alternately, Live365's targeted search capabilities allow you to quickly find stations that meet specific search criteria. If your mood changes, it is easy to switch to another channel—particularly if you have used the presets function to develop a collection of favorite stations.

If a great song catches your notice, a quick glance at the online playlist will tell you the song, artist, and album/CD name. To bookmark a song for future ref-erence, all you have to do is click on the ⊞ icon located to the right of the displayed song name. This will add the song to your WISHLIST for future refer-ence. Clicking on the BUY button to the left of the track information will allow you to buy the CD on Amazon.com, if available. If you use the Macintosh ver-sion of Live365's premium *Radio365* player, you'll also have the option of buy-ing the track as a download from the iTunes Music Store. See Chapter 11 for a profile of the iTunes Music Store.

Figure 2.1. Live365 Player Window

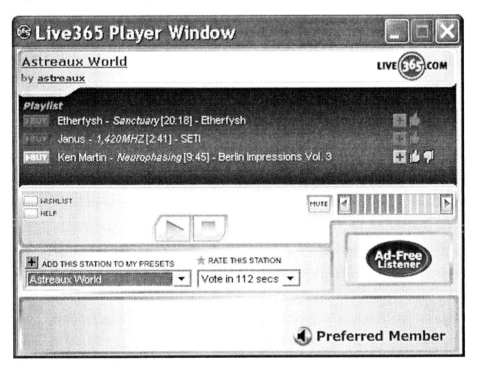

Free and Fee-Based Options

Live365 can be accessed for free, but registration is required. Periodic advertisements are served up via Web-based "pop-up" ads and audio ads. Once you have registered, you can customize your radio settings and maintain a personal list of radio "presets."

Live365 also offers a "VIP Preferred Member" option that provides ad-free listening, and access to more stations and better quality (MP3PRO encoded) music streams. VIP members can also use Live365's premium player software, *Radio365*. A no-commitment, one month VIP membership costs $5.95. A three-month subscription costs $4.95 per month, and increasing discounts are offered for increasing commitment levels: six months at $4.45 per month; twelve months at $3.95 per month; and twenty-four months at $3.65 per month.

A third option is to buy the *Radio365* software for $14.95. This provides listeners who have no wish to buy a subscription the option of using the enhanced *Radio365* software. While these users still have to listen to audio ads, they are spared the pop-up ads that non-subscribing Web users have to put up with.

Free trials are available for both the VIP Preferred Member subscriptions and the *Radio365* software.

One Drawback

The main strength of Live365—its huge body of grass roots, Internet enthusiast broadcasters—is also the source of its main weakness: the uneven quality of programming. Detractors have likened it to an Internet version of public access television, lacking in the polish and professionalism of commercial broadcasts. Most of these stations broadcast looping playlists. Listen long enough and you'll start hearing the same songs. The better stations have longer playlists and change them frequently. Live365 has addressed this issue by allowing listeners to rate stations. Stations which are highly rated *and* popular tend to be safer bets. You also have the option of browsing stations designated as PROFESSIONAL, which include the bigger, professionally programmed stations, as well as the college radio stations.

Tips for Using Live365

- **Start with Editor's Picks**
  The "Editor's Pick" designation is given to stations that impress Live365 staff as being particularly good. With so many stations to choose from, this feature helps you narrow down the choices. You can either browse EDITORS PICK'S or use the ADVANCED SEARCH bar to limit a keyword search to EDITORS PICK'S stations.

- **Take advantage of the presets feature**
  With such a rich directory it doesn't take much time to find stations of interest. Add these to your presets list. This makes it easy to find them later and gives you a quick menu of options whenever your mood changes and you want to listen to different music. Can't decide what to play? Click on the PLAY RANDOM button, and the system will pick one of your presets at random.

- **Try a type of music you've never heard before**
  The mind-boggling variety and specificity of music types available on Live365 makes it highly likely that you will come across stations for types of music you've never heard before. Click on the PLAY button ◀ and try them out! Or add them to your presets so you can try them later.

- **Use the wishlist feature to keep track of great songs**
  If a great song catches your notice, this is an easy way to "bookmark" that song so that you can remember it in the future.

- **Use keyword search to find specialized stations**
  The approximately 60 genre categories only begin to describe the variety to be found in the Live365 directory. If, for instance, you want to listen to bagpipe music, then enter the keyword "bagpipe" into the search box.

- **Learn more about stations using the Broadcaster's Profile**
  Many station listings have a Broadcaster's Profile icon (▣). Click on this icon to learn more about the station. Also, a link is often provided to an external Web site maintained by the broadcaster.

- **Check out the stations voted "Best of Live365" for 2004**
  "Mikey" awards have been handed out in 45 categories, including awards by genre and size of station, as well as a number of "special" awards. The list can be browsed at: http://www.live365.com/community/awards_winners.html

Getting Started

You will need to register with Live365 (http://www.live365.com) and configure a media player capable of playing MP3 streams using the instructions provided. If you have a Windows PC, choose the *Player365* option. If you have a Macintosh PC, choose the *iTunes* player option. These are the free player options. If you decide to become a VIP Preferred Member, you will have the option of using *Radio365*, their premium player (available for both Windows and Macintosh users).

See Chapter 27, *Live365 Discovery Plan*, for a detailed seven-day plan showing you how to get up-to-speed with Live365, and get the most out of its features.

Systems Requirements – Windows

- Windows 95, 98, ME, NT, 2000, XP
- Pentium class PC 300Mhz or higher
- Microsoft Internet Explorer 5.0 or higher

Systems Requirements – Macintosh

- Mac OS 8 or later (Mac OS 10.2 or later to use the *Radio365* player)
- 603 processor 100 MHz or faster (G3 or G4 processor recommended)
- 256 MB RAM and 500 MB free disk space
- Safari 1.0 or higher **or** Microsoft Internet Explorer 5.0 or higher

---

The Power of Thematic Radio

If music is the soundtrack to our lives, then as producers we've been given a powerful new tool: thematic radio stations. These stations play music to support a mood, an activity, or the feeling of being in a particular place or time. Need calming, background music to work to? Perhaps some upbeat music to help you get through a workout? Or how about some Irish pub music to listen to while drinking with your friends? The Internet radio service that has done the most with this concept is MSN Radio (http://entertainment.msn.com/stations). Their thematic stations are grouped into categories such as *For the Workplace, Let's Drink, Let's Make Love*, and *Workout Stations*. Within each category are stations that provide variations on the theme. Take the *Let's Eat* category: stations include French Bistro, Lowrider BBQ, and Taqueria Jukebox. Look for more services to experiment with thematic stations.

Live365 Summary

Pros

- The richest source of Internet radio stations under one umbrella
- Directory that allows targeted searching and browsing of stations
- Free (ad-supported) and fee-based (ad-free) options
- Personalization features: presets, song ratings, and the wishlist feature
- Rich community of broadcasters
- Available on Windows and Macintosh computers

Cons

- Uneven quality of amateur programs
- The large number of stations may overwhelm some people

Best for

- People looking for the biggest variety of programming
- Those with eclectic tastes
- People wanting to experience grassroots programming on the Internet
- People wanting to create their own radio stations

3

MSN Radio
A Toolbox for Music Exploration

Whereas Live365 can be likened to a large, teeming bazaar—with its huge collection of independent broadcasters—Microsoft's MSN Radio resembles more a large department store—orderly, well-lit, and stocked with goods to suit the majority of shoppers. While its 200+ stations don't provide the variety that Live365's 5,000+ stations do, they are easier to navigate. Because MSN Radio's programming is centrally managed, each station fits a specific niche, so you don't have the genre overlap that you do with Live365, where hundreds of stations are devoted to popular genres like Classic Rock and Hip Hop. But that's the trade-off. You are exchanging the chaos and variety that Live365's big community of broadcasters brings to table, for a more orderly environment, where the listener has more control over what gets played.

This control falls short of the personalization offered by a personalized radio service like LAUNCHcast (see Chapter 6), but exceeds that provided by Live365. Unlike Live365, MSN Radio has a skip button, which lets you skip songs, and a pause button. Like Live365, MSN Radio lets you create a station presets list and a wishlist of music for future reference (here called MY FAVORITES).

Likewise, there are free and fee-based versions of the service. The free version offers about 60 stations streamed at a low bit-rate ("AM quality"), and comes with frequent pitches to upgrade to the premium service, MSN Radio Plus. MSN Radio Plus provides 200+ ad-free stations, "near CD quality" streams, and the ability to use MSN's unique SoundsLike feature, which lets you generate stations which "sound like" a particular song, album, or artist.

Music Discovery with MSN Radio

Where MSN Radio really distinguishes itself is in the tools it provides the music explorer. First, there is the rich selection of radio stations. Second, there are links to music information: reviews, biographies, discographies, and genre information. These links are displayed for each song, as it is being played, in the NOW PLAYING display on the MSN Radio player. Clicking on one of these links will open a corresponding page in a separate Web browser window. If you click on the artist's name, an artist information Web page will open. If you click on the album name, an album Web page will open. Click on the album name, an album Web page will open. This information is provided by AMG, the publisher of the Allmusic Web site. From these Web pages, MSN Radio gives you the option of playing a "SoundsLike" radio station, based on a given artist, album, or song. This lets you tell MSN Radio to, "play more like this."

Having used these tools to identify new music of interest, you can capture this information to a MY FAVORITES list, where you can revisit it later, to do further research or make a purchase. Station choices can be browsed on the MSN Radio Stations Web page (http://entertainment.msn.com/stations) or in the player using the RADIO TUNER tab.

MSN Radio also allows listeners to write music reviews, but thus far I haven't found them very numerous or useful. Similarly, MSN Radio lets you rate music, but these ratings don't have any immediate impact on the programming. To learn about a service in which ratings do have an immediate impact on programming, see Chapter 6, *LAUNCHcast: Your Own Personal Station*.

Figure 3.1. MSN Radio Player

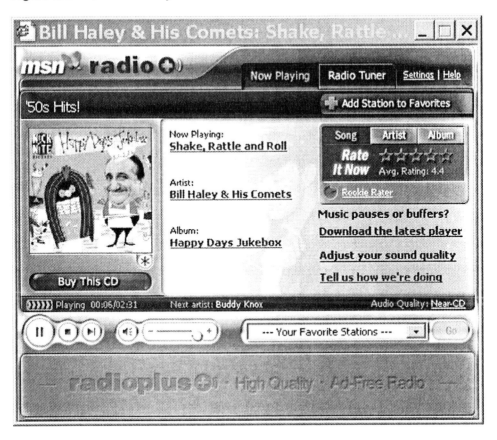

Access Options

The free MSN Radio service requires that you register with Microsoft and provides access to approximately 60 stations.

MSN Radio Plus costs $4.99 per month or $29.99 per year. Subscribers receive exclusive access to 140 more stations, including all the theme and mood based stations, the use of the SoundsLike feature, ad-free listening, and access to higher quality music streams. A generous one-month free trial is offered.

As of this writing, subscribers also get free access to Major League Baseball Gameday Audio broadcasts, for which separate registration is required. MSN Radio Plus is only available to those with a U.S. credit card and a U.S billing address.

Getting Started

Go to the MSN Radio Web page (http://entertainment.msn.com/stations) and click on one of the radio station listings. You will be prompted to login with a Microsoft Passport ID. If you don't have one, you will be given the option of creating one and associating it with your existing e-mail address. Once this has been completed, and you have accepted their terms and conditions, you will be able to play MSN Radio. At this point you also have the option of signing up for a one-month trial of MSN Radio Plus, which requires that you submit your credit card information. Your card will be charged if you fail to cancel the account before the trial period is over.

See Chapter 28, *MSN Radio Discovery Plan,* for a detailed seven-day plan showing you how to get up-to-speed with MSN Radio, and get the most out of its features.

System Requirements

- Windows 98/ME/2000/XP
- Windows Media Player 7.0 or higher (9.0 recommended)
- Internet Explorer 5.0 or higher

Tips for Using MSN Radio

- **Sign up for the free trial of MSN Radio Plus**
  MSN Radio Plus offers a lot more than the free service. Take advantage of the generous one month trial and see if it's worth it. Mark down the trial end-date on your calendar so that you can cancel without being charged.

- **Create Internet shortcuts (bookmarks) to Favorites pages**
  Put a shortcut to your MY FAVORITE STATIONS Web page on your desktop. This way you can quickly pull up your list of favorite stations, pick one, and start listening immediately. Shortcuts to your other MY FAVORITES pages (albums, artists, songs) can also be helpful.

- **Clicking on a station name will launch the station**
  If you are playing a station and browsing other station options on the Web page, be aware that clicking on a station name won't get you more information about that station, it will simply launch it and preempt the station that is currently playing.

- **Explore the genre pages on the MSN Music Web site**
  At the bottom of each artist information page on the MSN Music Web site is a section titled RELATED MUSIC STYLES AND STATIONS. Here you will find links to music style or genre pages, on which you will find lists of key artists and albums within that style, as well radio stations that relate to that style.

- **Try the theme and mood stations (MSN Radio Plus only)**
  Sample the FOR THE WORKPLACE stations and see if any of the stations would be good to work to.

- **Use Amazon.com to access listener written reviews**
  MSN Radio's listener written reviews are pretty sparse. So if you're looking for such reviews, use Amazon.com's customer reviews instead. There is usually a BUY IT FROM AMAZON link right on the MSN album information page, which will take you to Amazon.com, where you can read their reviews.

MSN Radio Pitfalls

- **Song and Album "Favorites" lists are awkward to use**
  MSN Radio doesn't let you designate favorite songs or albums using the player. You have to go to a separate Web page to do this. The same applies when you want to access these "favorites" lists.

- **Available stations are missing from the station listings**
  Some stations I found using the genre information pages (e.g., British Folk) were not listed on the Radio Stations Web page.

MSN Radio Summary

Pros

- Rich selection of radio stations
- "SoundsLike" stations let you "get more music like this"
- Rich music information from the Allmusic guide
- Free (ad-supported) and fee-based (ad-free) options
- Ability to pause and skip songs

Cons

- Available only to Windows users

Best for

- Listeners who prefer an interactive radio service
- Those attracted to MSN's music discovery tools
- Existing MSN Users
- Baseball fans (to get free access to Major League Gameday Broadcasts)

4

Other Internet Radio Services

Beyond Live365 and MSN Radio, there are other stand-alone Internet radio services worth knowing about. These are highlighted below. Another kind of Internet radio service, the personalized radio service, will be discussed in the next three chapters. A number of on-demand music services discussed in later chapters also provide Internet radio offerings. Generally speaking, however, these offerings aren't as rich as those of the best stand-alone services.

BBC Radio (http://www.bbc.co.uk/radio)

- Provides 16 stations of free, U.K. based radio programming
- Broadcasts U.K. Record Chart shows
- Archived shows are available

The Iceberg (http://www.theiceberg.com)

- Provides free, ad-supported access to 200+ music stations from Canada
- Provides Music Yearbook channels, which play hits from a specific year
- Registration required

Moontaxi Radio (http://www.moontaxi.com/Portal/Home.aspx)

- Provides a wide variety of genre-based stations and hosted programs
- Basic plan is free and provides 5 channels of music
- Basic Plus ($1.99/month or $19.99/year) provides 100+ channels
- "Supersonic" plan ($2.99/month or $29.99/year) provides 150+ channels of ad-free programming as well as high fidelity streams
- Windows Media Player 9 is required to use the high fidelity streams

NetRadio.com (http://www.netradio.com)

- Provides ad-free jazz and classical programming (seven channels)
- Cost is $4.95/month or $36.50/year; a 30-day free trial is offered
- Emphasizes high-quality, expert programming
- Subscribers get access to written materials provided by programmers
- For Windows users; a Macintosh version is planned

Radio@AOL / Radio @Netscape (http://radio.netscape.com)

- Provides America Online (AOL) users access to approximately 175 stations
- Links to artist biographies, discographies, and reviews are provided
- Radio@Netscape is a limited version available to non-AOL users, used primarily to sell AOL subscriptions
- For Windows users only

Radio Free Virgin (http://www.radiofreevirgin.com)

- Provides Windows users free access to approximately 30 stations
- Provides fee-based access to 60+ stations, ad-free ($4.95/month)
- Provides high quality audio streams to fee-based users
- Includes: Grammy's Channel, Rolling Stone Channel, Playboy Channel

RadioIO (http://www.radioio.com)

- Provides 19 channels covering rock, pop, classical, jazz, and world music
- Features disc jockeys (called "streamHosts") who will take your requests
- An Internet music search engine provides access to music information
- Streams are offered in Windows Media, Real Audio, Quicktime, and MP3 formats to accommodate a wide range of player software
- Free plan offers 11 channels streaming at a low bit rate ("amQuality")
- A $2.99/month subscription expands this to 19 channels; for $5.99/month you upgrade to "fmQuality" streams; for $9.99/month, you get "cdQuality" streams

5

Personalized Radio
You're in the Driver's Seat

If you want to influence what gets played on traditional radio you have the option of calling in a song request to the disc jockey (DJ). Or, if the station is more technically savvy, you can send requests by fax, e-mail, or instant messenger. This, of course, presumes that the show is live and the DJ is available to review your request—which is often not the case. Most Internet radio stations are similar in this regard: your ability to influence the playlist is limited, and your main choice is whether to listen or not. The Internet is a two-way medium, however, and a number of services have emerged to exploit this fact. As a listener you get some control over the broadcast.

At its most basic, this control includes the ability to skip or pause songs that you are listening to. At its most sophisticated, personalized radio allows you to fine tune a broadcast based on a profile of your musical preferences. This can range from genre preferences (I like Classical but I don't like Rap) to artist and album preferences (I like David Bowie but not his latest album), and song preferences (I like the original version of *The Night They Drove Old Dixie Down*).

Some personalized radio services work by letting you type in the name of artists that interest you. The resulting music stream, or "station", will deliver music by these and related artists. In some cases, you can specify artists to exclude from your station. Some services let you specify the genres that interest you, while others let you listen to music from a specific year. Depending on the service, preferences can either be stated up-front, as in the process of configuring a station and then listening to it, or they can be refined over time, as in the process of rating songs while you listen to them. At least one service lets you do both. While listening to music on some services, one option is to say, in effect, "Get me more music like this." A chosen song, artist, or album is then used to automatically generate a playlist of related music.

While personalized radio requires more effort than simply selecting a station and listening, the payoff is well worth it—especially for people who want more control over what they listen to. The process can be addictive!

Why Personalized Radio Matters

Personalized radio can be thought of as "near on-demand" radio, because listener selections will eventually show up on their station playlist. As such, it is the poor man's on-demand service, providing many of the benefits of a true on-demand music service for less money.

While personalized radio does not allow you to control the exact composition or sequence of your playlist—for this you need a true on-demand music service—it does help you control the content of your station. In many situations this is all you need—especially if your intent is to discover new music. Personalized radio combines the serendipity and surprise of radio with the ability to steer towards the kind of music that interests you at any given moment. This means you are more likely to hear songs that you want to hear, and have a more productive listening experience. Personalized radio gives you the means to follow a musical trail—using favored songs or artists as "scent."

Suppose you hear a great song, from an artist you've never heard of before, and you want to hear more like it. You could go out and buy the album containing the song, but that costs a lot of money. What's more, the song might be an exception. Listening to the album might reveal that, for the most part, you don't like this artist's music. Personalized radio lets you economically find and sample "music like this", either by that artist or by related artists. Rather than passively receiving what someone else decides is good for you, you are shaping the radio program and drawing added satisfaction from any happy discoveries that result. This feeling of control can be very satisfying.

The next chapter will profile the best personalized radio service, LAUNCHcast. The following chapter will discuss other personalized radio offerings with notable or unique features.

6

LAUNCHcast
Your Own Personal Station

Available in free and fee-based versions, LAUNCHcast provides a personalized music stream based on music that you rate. Upon signing up, you are asked to enter the names of favorite artists and select music genres that interest you, after which songs will start playing. As each song plays you have the option of rating it, which in turn influences what songs will be served to you subsequently. Other options include pausing a song or skipping it. For each song it is possible to rate the song, the album the song is on, and/or the artist on a scale from four stars (can't get enough) to zero stars (never play again). This last option—to ban music from your station—is beloved by legions of devoted LAUNCHcast users. For many, it signifies freedom from the tyranny of force fed, Top-40 music programming. The more songs you rate, the better your profile becomes, and the more likely you are to enjoy what gets played on your station.

LAUNCHcast also provides approximately 50 pre-programmed stations, as well as "fan stations," which focus on the music of one artist plus the music of related artists. Music on these stations can also be rated, and these ratings are incorporated into your personal station profile. In addition, LAUNCHcast also offers a large collection of music videos.

Music Discovery with LAUNCHcast

While you are listening to LAUNCHcast, you can access music information by clicking on the linked names of artists, songs, and albums within the player window. This information can include biographies, reviews, discographies, and in some cases news, photos, interviews, lyrics, and links to other artist related Web sites. Artist pages also provide links to fan stations, in case you want to listen to more of their music, as well as links to the personal stations of fans of that artist.

Listening to the stations of other listeners lets you try their favorite music. This feature also makes you into a disc jockey of sorts, with your "program" available to others. A SHARE THIS STATION option makes it easy to tell friends about your station.

Communication with other fans is possible using Yahoo Instant Messenger, artist-focused message boards, and a LAUNCHcast user group, also available on Yahoo. The user group is a place for users to discuss new features, make suggestions, air complaints, and discuss issues with LAUNCHcast product management. Being a subscriber to this list, I have seen lots of user enthusiasm as well as frank and open exchanges between users and LAUNCHcast product management.

Figure 6.1. LAUNCHcast player

Effort Is Required and Rewarded

LAUNCHcast is not for idle listeners, at least when it comes to developing the truly rich profile that LAUNCHcast is capable of providing. The music rating system, though rich, is complex and the implications of certain rating decisions are not immediately clear to new users. It takes time to develop a personal station, but watching it take shape and grow can be very satisfying. The process is highly involving and, for some, addictive.

Premium Option - LAUNCHcast Plus

As of this writing $3.99 per month or $35.99 per year will get you:

- **Ad-free listening**

- **Unlimited use of your personal station**
  The free version of LAUNCHcast restricts you to playing 800 songs on your personal station per month.

- **Higher quality music streams and unlimited skipping**
  The free version of LAUNCHcast streams at "medium" quality, and after the first 800 songs per month, downgrades the stream to "low" quality and disables the song skipping feature. Premium subscribers get unlimited access to "high quality" streams and song skipping.

- **More pre-programmed music stations** (approximately 80 more)

- **Moods**
  These are filtered versions of your personal station which restrict the playlist to specific genres of your choosing. A "mood" also lets you determine the proportion of unrated music that gets played (versus music that you have already rated).

- **Influencers**
  Here you can "subscribe" to other people's LAUNCHcast stations, letting their ratings influence your playlist. These stations are called "influencers."

LAUNCHcast Plus is available in the U.S. and Canada. The free LAUNCHcast service is available worldwide.

Getting Started

To use LAUNCHcast, you will need a Yahoo ID, which can be freely obtained by signing up via the LAUNCHcast Web site (http://radio.yahoo.com). The LAUNCHcast player relies on Windows Media Player, Macromedia Flash, and a Web browser to work, so these must be installed. If you have a Windows PC, it's more than likely your system will meet these requirements. Support for the Macintosh, while available, is more limited.

See Chapter 29, *LAUNCHcast Discovery Plan*, for a detailed seven-day plan showing you how to get up-to-speed with LAUNCHcast, and get the most out of its features.

System Requirements - Windows PCs

- Windows 95, 98, ME, NT 4.0, 2000, XP
- Pentium II, 233MHz or faster, and at least 64MB RAM
- Internet Explorer, Netscape, or AOL browser, all at 4.0 or higher
- Windows Media Player 6.4 or higher
- Macromedia Flash 4.0 or higher

System Requirements - Macintosh

- Mac OS 8.5 to 9.2.2 (OS X not supported)
- 200MHz PowerPC (iMac OK)
- 64MB RAM
- Netscape Navigator 4.5 to 4.7 *only*
- Windows Media Player 7.01 or higher
- Macromedia Flash 4.0 or higher

Once you are signed in, it is simply a matter of making some initial music preference choices, after which music will start playing and you can begin rating music and building your station. There is a setting for blocking songs with explicit lyrics, if that is your wish.

Tips for Using LAUNCHcast

- **Rate lots of music**
  The more music you rate, the more closely your station will match your tastes. Make sure that you use the genre and subgenre rating menu to tune the overall genre mix that gets served to you. You can also rate music on the RECENTLY PLAYED MUSIC page or the ARTIST and DISCOGRAPHY pages. More information on the rating scheme can be found in the help files.

- **Remember that higher rated music will play more frequently**
  Just because I love an old song doesn't mean I want to hear it played frequently (and risk wearing it out). So rather than think about the ratings as a referendum on how good songs/artists/albums are, consider them an indicator of how frequently you want that music to be played. Note that your feelings can change over time, and it's easy to revise ratings in either direction.

- **To focus on one artist and related music use the "fan stations"**
  From either the LAUNCHcast home page or your MY STATION Web page,
  search for an artist and then go to the artist Web page. Once there, click
  on the listen icon [LISTEN] for the fan station. Fan stations are not available for all artists.

- **Preview newly released albums using LAUNCHcast**
  Your favorite artist just released a new album and you're not quite ready
  to buy it. Seek it out on LAUNCHcast and—assuming it's been added to
  the system—rate it highly and then wait for songs from the album to start
  playing.

- **Understand why you have been served a song**
  LAUNCHcast always tells you why you've been served a song. The answer
  will be one of the following:

  -You rated the song [song name]

  -You rated this genre

  -You rated [artist name]

  -This song is recommended for you

  -This song is popular on LAUNCHcast stations (other than yours)

About LAUNCHcast

LAUNCHcast is part of Yahoo's Launch music portal, which provides access to
music videos, news, reviews, charts, free downloads, and other promotional
information. In February 2004, LAUNCHcast had 2.8 million listeners according to the Arbitron ratings. LAUNCHcast began operations early in 2000. Its
parent company, Launch Media, was bought by Yahoo in late 2001 and
LAUNCHcast was integrated with Yahoo's Music offering. People who use
Yahoo's other services can now use the same ID to access LAUNCHcast.

LAUNCHcast Summary

Pros

- Allows users to create a finely tuned personal radio station
- Provides the richest personalization of any Internet radio service
- Provides strong community features that encourage sharing of music
- Provides a "near on-demand" alternative to more expensive, on-demand music services

Cons

- Requires more effort to use than other Internet radio services
- Free version of personal station will only play 800 songs per month
- No support for Macintosh OS X users

Best for

- People wanting maximum control over what they hear via Internet radio
- People interested in creating and sharing a personal radio station
- Budget-conscious listeners

7

Other Personalized Radio Services

Beyond LAUNCHcast, there are other services with personalization capabilities worth noting. These include:

- **Musicmatch Radio** - http://www.musicmatch.com
  Musicmatch Radio lets you listen to stations based on artist, era (year or decade), and genre preferences. You also have the option of entering artist preferences and making your *Musicmatch Jukebox* play logs available to fuel Musicmatch's "Music Discovery Engine," which supplies music recommendations. A free, ad-supported version of the service is available, with 200 stations. Two fee-based radio options are also available: Premium Radio ($2.95 per month, billed annually) and Platinum Radio ($4.95 per month, billed annually). Both of these options allow full access to all personalization features. The Platinum Radio option lets you play contiguous blocks of music from chosen artists, a "near on-demand" feature that is unique to Musicmatch. Musicmatch's offerings are profiled in more detail in Chapter 13. Free trials are available. For Windows PC users only.

- **MyMoontaxi** - http://my.moontaxi.ca
  Targeted at jazz and classical music aficionados, this service lets you create up to three personal channels or playlists. Each playlist can be populated with songs identified using a search tool or by browsing playlists created by Moontaxi editors and other subscribers. Songs can also be added from featured albums and best-of lists (e.g., Gramophone Top 100) posted by the editors. Once created, these playlists can be edited, ordered and shuffled. Individual songs can be played on-demand which is a notable feature. Pre-programmed stations from the Moontaxi radio service (covered in Chapter 4) are also available. Available to both Windows PC and Macintosh users, this service costs $4.95 per month or $49.95 per year. Free trials are available.

- **Accuradio** - http://www.accuradio.com
  Accuradio, whose tagline is "Internet radio you can control," provides access to 17 channels and over 120 sub-channels. Accuradio allows you to review a collection of artists or styles included in a channel, and de-select up to five that you'd like to exclude from the mix. For example, there is a Broadway Music channel that features music from currently running

shows. The control panel lists all the shows being played and then allows you to de-select any you'd rather not hear played (e.g., the *Lion King*). For Windows PC users. This service is free.

- **Epitonic Radio** - http://epitonic.com/radio.jsp
  With this promotional radio service, you configure a playlist by selecting which of 50 different genres of music you'd like to hear from and specifying how many tracks you want played (20, 50, 100, or 500). It's simple and effective. This is a great place to hear new music. Available for Windows PC and Macintosh users. This service is free.

- **Microsoft's MSN Radio Plus** - http://entertainment.msn.com/stations
  Although MSN Radio Plus has already been covered in Chapter 3, it should be noted that its SoundsLike feature is interactive in that it lets you generate SoundsLike stations based on a given artist, album, or song. In effect, it allows you to tell the service, "Get me more music like this."

The on-demand services Rhapsody and Napster (discussed in Chapters 9 and 14) also provide personalized radio subscription options, both separately and as part of their higher priced on-demand subscriptions. In each case, these services let subscribers create custom stations based on their artist preferences.

8

Online Jukeboxes
Unlimited Listening for a Flat Fee

> Digital music evangelists talk a lot about a gadget they like to call the "celestial jukebox." In layman terms, this is a networked device that will allow you to download any song your heart desires, anytime. Imagine a Walkman that had broadband wireless connectivity to the Net, could access the entire world's catalog of recorded music and played back that music with impeccable sound quality. You would be able to plug this into your stereo or speakers, or listen to it in your car.
>
> Janelle Brown, "The Jukebox Manifesto", *Salon* (Nov. 13, 2000).

Imagine having the world's music at your fingertips. With one click, any recording you desired would be retrieved, delivered, and played, hassle-free and for a reasonable price. This vision of the Celestial Jukebox has been inspiring people ever since Napster first broke on to the scene and gave millions a taste—however flawed—of what it might be like. While the new music services still fall short of the ideal, they offer tremendous value to music lovers looking for on-demand access to large catalogs of music.

A Day in the Life

So what is it like to have an enormous library of music at your fingertips? The first word that comes to mind is freedom—the freedom to roam about and to play music without worrying about how it's going to hit your wallet. Online jukeboxes with flat-fee subscription plans make this possible. It's easy to be adventuresome when there is no incremental cost for trying a new album. I've been using the Rhapsody music service for over a year now and have used it to seek out music I'd heard about, but had never sought out.

Take Bob Dylan, for example. I'd been running into Dylan fans for years. I had listened to songs of his here and there on the radio, but had never bought an album (true confession). When I logged in one day, the NEWLY ADDED ALBUMS page on Rhapsody informed me that Dylan's famous album *Blonde on Blonde* had just been added. I played it and found it quite good. I then played his latest effort, *Love and Theft*, and enjoyed that as well. If I had to buy the CDs in order to try this music I probably wouldn't have. Multiply this by the scores of artists that have deserved my attention over the years and not gotten it—

and I see an opportunity to cover a lot of worthy musical ground. Conversely, it's just as easy to try music I'm sure I won't like—certain Top 40 music, for example—if only to say I've given it a fair chance. If I'm pleasantly surprised, so much the better.

On another day, while working at my PC, I was struck by an impulse to listen to some harpsichord music. By searching for the key word "harpsichord" in the ALBUM TITLE field on Rhapsody, I came up with over ten records of harpsichord music. I spent the next hour or two happily working away while the orderly, metallic sounds of the harpsichord kept me company. This is what it's about: musical whims and impulses that can be pursued on the spur of the moment without the angst of a purchase decision getting in the way. In the end, this is perhaps the most revolutionary option in digital music today: unlimited listening for a fixed price.

On-demand music services provide two ways of delivering music: online jukeboxes and downloading services. With online jukeboxes, you select the music you want and hit the play button; music will then stream to your computer and play through your speakers or headphones. Or, if you have the right setup, through your stereo or home entertainment system. For this reason, they are also called streaming services. Easy to use, online jukeboxes don't require you to worry about how the music is organized or stored, something that is an issue with downloaded music

Pay to Play

Online jukebox services provide "all you can drink" access to a huge library of music for a monthly fee, usually around ten dollars. You can listen to as many songs and albums as you like, provided your subscription is current. It's like cable TV. If you stop paying your monthly fee, your access goes away.

For heavy listeners and the musical explorer it is a great deal. The catch is that you have to be connected to the Internet in order to listen to the music. Anything less than a broadband connection (e.g., cable modem or DSL) will not be suitable. Dial-up connections are too slow.

If you spend numerous hours in close proximity to a broadband connection, at work or at home, then you should strongly consider trying an online jukebox service. A downloading option is usually available as well, allowing you to purchase songs and make them portable. Major services offering an online jukebox option include Rhapsody, Musicmatch, and Napster.

Beyond Ownership

Of course, not everybody is thrilled at the idea of renting music. The idea takes some getting used to. But it does have advantages. Consider the alternative. Suppose you had a personal collection of 10,000 CDs, yours to play whenever you wanted. Sounds great, doesn't it? But think for a moment. Where would you put them? How would you find the one that you wanted to play? How could you tell when one was missing?

One of the benefits of an online jukebox service is that somebody else takes care of storing the music, organizing it, and securing it from harm. These are things you have to do when managing your own digital music collection. Add search capabilities and rich music information, and the idea of centrally managed music starts to look pretty good. Also, it's a lot cheaper than owning music. For ten dollars per month, you get access to more albums than you could ever afford to buy. And even if you aren't ready to give up the idea of owning music, these services will help you get your money's worth. By letting you play songs and albums prior to buying them, they ensure that you know what you're getting.

Why It's Taking So Long to Assemble the Celestial Jukebox

Perhaps you've noticed your favorite records still aren't available on a legitimate online music service. It could be the copyright owners aren't happy with the terms the music service is offering. Or it could simply be that the long, and often tortuous process of tracking down copyright owners and negotiating licenses has yet to run its course. For each song, this involves negotiating with both the owners of the composition *and* the owners of the recording. Records documenting these ownership rights are scattered across an alphabet soup of agencies and record labels. Older records are in paper files. Various agents and intermediaries have to be dealt with. You get the picture. This explains the Swiss cheese effect you get when browsing certain albums on a service like Rhapsody. Some songs are available, whereas others are not. Expect this situation to improve over time.

Online Music Discovery

Consider the following scenarios:

- You've read an album review in the newspaper that intrigues you, and now you want to listen to the album.

- You've just seen a movie with a great soundtrack and you'd like to learn more about the music.

- You've heard a great song on the radio, and you'd like to hear more music by the same artist.

- It's December, and the annual "best album" lists have been published by music critics.

- You've heard reference to a piece of music in a conversation, an article, or an interview. You think you'd like to hear it.

- The Grammy Award nominees have been announced. You'd like the preview the music so you can decide for yourself who should win.

Much of the time, you'll find what you are looking for. A service like Rhapsody puts over 58,000 albums at your disposal, with more being added daily. With a rich historical archive of music at your disposal, you can also become acquainted with important artists and styles of music from earlier eras. Thus, the online jukebox service becomes a tool for increasing your knowledge of music. In addition, published music guides take on a new usefulness, because now you can listen to records while you read about them.

Narrowing Down the Choices

Consider these factors when looking at online jukebox offerings:

- **Will it work with my computer?**
  Rhapsody, Musicmatch On-Demand, and Napster require software that only runs on Windows PCs. Streamwaves uses a Web interface, and works on both Windows PCs and Macintosh OS X systems.

- **How good is the catalog?**
  Pay attention not only to the size of the catalog, but also to its scope. What types of artists and music are included? If you are mainly interested in classical music or jazz, check the coverage in these areas.

- **Are there multiple ways to find music of interest?**
  Does the interface provide rich avenues into the catalog? Does the service help you discover new music?

- **How good is the artist and music information provided?**
  What does the service provide in the way of album reviews, artist and genre information, and music recommendations?

- **What downloading options are available?**
  Are there options for making music portable? How easy are they? Will they work with my jukebox software or portable music player? How much does it cost?

- **How do playlists work?**
  Can you create, edit, save, and reuse song playlists? Is it easy to do? Can you share playlists with other subscribers?

- **How good is the Internet radio offering?**
  All the major jukebox offerings come with ad-free radio stations. Are the stations choices and programming good? It is easy to jump back and forth between listening to the radio and playing something on the jukebox?

The next chapter discusses Rhapsody, which to my thinking is the best online jukebox service. Other online jukebox services are discussed in Chapters 13 and 14. These include offerings from Musicmatch and Napster, both of which combine an online jukebox with a downloading service and the jukebox software necessary to the manage the resulting digital music collection.

9

Rhapsody
A Near-Celestial Jukebox

Better than any other service, RealNetwork's Rhapsody has captured the promise of on-demand music. For a flat fee, Rhapsody subscribers have unlimited access to a large catalog of major label and independent music. For $0.79 per track, users can burn selected tracks to CDs in CD audio format, making them playable in any CD player and available for "ripping" into MP3 files as well. Add to this a set of premium Internet radio stations, and the ability to create customized radio stations, and you have an impressive online music offering. This service is only available in the United States.

The player software that comes with Rhapsody is well designed, providing good sound quality and a good interface for browsing and music discovery, one that significantly adds to the value of the service. Unfortunately it is available only for Windows PCs. Upon logging in, users will see a search box, a music genre browsing menu, and music that is currently being highlighted by Rhapsody's editorial staff, including a featured album, a radio station, and a featured playlist devoted to a particular theme. Also visible are a list of the most popular artists on Rhapsody and a list of JUST ADDED ALBUMS. Photographs and album art add to the display. Other features include:

- **My Library**
  Bookmark songs, albums, and radio stations for later use. You can also create and save playlists—either for playing or for CD burning. You can access your library from any PC that has Rhapsody software loaded on it.

- **Playlist Sharing**
  Send playlist links by e-mail to other subscribers. When they click on the link, the playlist will load into their Rhapsody player. These playlist links can also be posted to Web pages or blogs.

- **Keyboard Shortcuts**
  Keyboard equivalents exist for all commands (e.g., Ctrl-P to play or pause).

- **User Settings**
  Here you can enable a mini-player that takes up less screen space, and control certain behaviors such as auto-login on startup or what happens when you click on the PLAY NOW icon.

Figure 9.1. Rhapsody Player

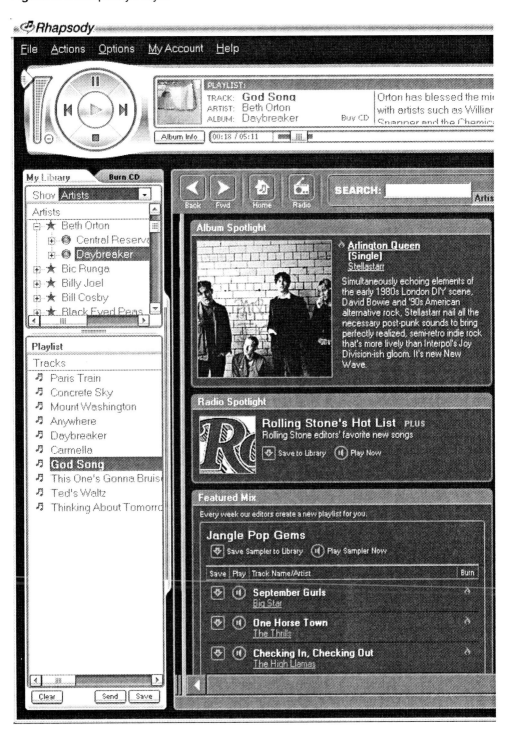

Music Discovery with Rhapsody

As far as music discovery is concerned, an on-demand music catalog is only as good as the paths provided into it. Luckily for us, Rhapsody has done an excellent job here.

If you know an artist, song, or album you'd like to search for, you can use the search feature to check on availability. A perusal of the JUST ADDED ALBUMS list can alert you to new music of interest, as can highlighted albums, mixes, and radio stations.

Genre Information

The BROWSE GENRES menu opens up lots of other options. Each genre page offers the following opportunities:

Learn More About the Genre

- GENRE SPOTLIGHT   A brief description of the genre
- GENRE SAMPLE MIX   A representative mix of tracks
- SUBGENRES   Links to similar pages focused on subgenres
- RADIO STATIONS   Rhapsody Radio stations that play this genre

Identify Important Artists in the Genre

- KEY ARTISTS LIST   Notable figures in the evolution of this style
- MOST POPULAR ARTISTS   Based on Rhapsody usage
- BROWSE ALL ARTISTS   An alphabetical list of all artists in the genre

Find Albums / Recordings to Play

- JUST ADDED   Albums just added to the catalog
- KEY ALBUMS   Critically acclaimed releases

Unlike some other services, Rhapsody will highlight artists and albums that are critically acclaimed and not just those that are most popular with their customers.

Artist Information

Once you've found an artist page, you can review a one-paragraph artist snapshot and review a list of the artist's main releases and other recordings. Rhapsody displays both the releases it has the rights to play and those it doesn't have the rights to play. This helps you determine the strength of its holdings for that artist, and whether there are albums that you may need to pursue elsewhere. Also present are links to related artists, a sampler playlist, and radio stations which play that artist. Links to relevant genre information pages are also available. In some cases, there are links to videos. The RealPlayer software is required to view these.

My only complaint with Rhapsody is the skimpiness of the record and artist information. For albums you can't get much in the way of reviews or ratings. Without this information, the process of selecting records becomes more of a hit-or-miss affair. Therefore, I recommend that you use Rhapsody in conjunction with the free Allmusic Web site (http://www.allmusic.com/), which provides much of the information that Rhapsody lacks. For more information, consult Part Two, *Music Information on the Internet.*

Rhapsody Radio

When you hear a song you like on one of Rhapsody's radio stations, you have the option of clicking the album information button on the playlist. If the album is part of the on-demand listening collection, you then have the option of adding it to the MY LIBRARY area for later use. This is a great way to discover new albums of interest.

Rhapsody provides approximately 70 stations of commercial free radio and gives you the ability to create custom radio stations by entering the names of up to ten artists whose music you like. Rhapsody also has two "best music of the year" stations, one for 2002 and one for 2003, which feature music selected by Rhapsody's editorial staff.

The Catalog

As of September 27, 2004, Rhapsody's catalog contained:

36,906 artists
61,695 albums
776,394 tracks

Content from all Big 5 record labels is included: Universal Music Group, Sony Music Entertainment, EMI Group, Warner Brothers Music, and BMG Entertainment. Content from over 450 independent labels, including the Naxos Classical label, is also included. More specifics are available on the Rhapsody Web site at: http://www.rhapsody.com/music.jsp?sect=labels.

Access Options

There are three access and payment options for Rhapsody:

- **Rhapsody All Access**
  Provides unlimited access to streams, all Internet radio functionality, and the ability to burn CDs for $.79 per track, less than what a la carte services like the iTunes Music Store are charging. Cost: $9.95 per month.

- **Rhapsody Radio Plus**
  Provides access to Rhapsody's Internet and personalized radio offerings but not to the on-demand archive or CD-burning capabilities. Cost: $4.95 per month.

- **Rhapsody Preview**
  This no-cost option provides access to a limited number of free radio stations, and to 30-second clips from the Rhapsody music catalog.

Payment is by credit card. Free trials are offered, which allow you to try the full Rhapsody offering at no cost. Three-month "starter pack" certificates can be purchased at Best Buy stores and used as a gift. Periodically, Rhapsody runs specials and extended free trials to encourage people to sign up.

Getting Started

Go to the Rhapsody Web site (http://www.rhapsody.com/) and sign-up for a free trial of the All-Access plan. Follow the instructions for downloading and installing the Rhapsody player.

See Chapter 31, *Rhapsody Discovery Plan*, for a detailed seven-day plan showing you how to get up-to-speed with Rhapsody, and get the most out of its features.

System Requirements

- Windows XP, ME, 2000, 98SE, or NT 4.0 (Service Pack 6)
- Microsoft Internet Explorer 5.0 or later
- Pentium Class 300MHz processor or better with 64MB RAM
- 250 MB hard drive space

In addition, a CD burner needs to be connected to your computer if you wish to use Rhapsody's CD burning feature.

Tips for Using Rhapsody

- **Use the powerful music discovery tools available to you**
  As discussed above, the genre and artist pages allow for productive browsing of the catalog. Periodically browse the JUST ADDED ALBUMS page.

- **Use the Allmusic Web site to obtain more artist information**
  The Allmusic site will supply record details, ratings, reviews, and more detailed artist information. This will supplement the skimpy artist information provided by Rhapsody.

- **Use the VIEW ALL option when looking at a the list of releases**
  This handy feature will tell you what albums by a given artist Rhapsody does and *does not* have. Rhapsody is to be commended for being up front about what it doesn't have. In so doing it has turned a liability (revelation of the gaps in its catalog) into a plus.

- **Listen before burning**
  While this may seem obvious, it's worth listening to a track a few times before spending $0.79 to burn it to a CD. Your $0.79 is making the song portable. Ask yourself: do I really need to make this song portable?

- **Check used CD prices before burning an album**
  If you're willing to wait a bit, used CDs from online stores like Amazon.com can sometimes be cheaper than burning the album to CD.

- **Make a backup copy of any songs that you burn**
  Given the vagaries of CD burning and the questionable quality of some blank CD-R disks, it makes sense to make a backup copy of burned songs on your computer.

- **Recruit a friend to sign-up for Rhapsody All-Access**
  Then you can have fun e-mailing each other playlists of your favorite songs.

- **Click again on the HOME icon to see other highlighted albums**
  The editors highlight multiple albums at any one given time. By clicking on the home icon, you can cycle through current choices.

Rhapsody Pitfalls

Despite my warm recommendation, Rhapsody is not without drawbacks. A few to be aware of:

- **Missing Tracks**
Many albums on Rhapsody have tracks that are unavailable: these tracks are grayed out on the track listings. Permission has not been obtained to play these songs. A typical scenario involves an artist performing a song that was written by another artist. Thus, more than one copyright holder has to give permission. This leaves some album listings looking like Swiss cheese. For more information see the sidebar on page 45, "Why It's Taking So Long to Assemble the Celestial Jukebox." This is a problem that afflicts *all* the on-demand music services, not just Rhapsody.

- **Missing albums for an artist**
Using the VIEW ALL RELEASES option will indicate, that for many artists, only some of their albums are available. Again, there may be different copyright holders involved that have not given permission to use particular albums. Many artists record for different record labels during their career, which complicates the process of getting permissions to play all their music. Note that at least Rhapsody tells you which albums they don't have. Other services simply show you what they have, leaving you to guess at what you're missing.

- **Some tracks are not burnable**
Some copyright holders will allow a song to be played but not burned to CD. At present, 88% of Rhapsody's catalog is burnable. I expect this percentage to continue to increase over the next year or two.

About Rhapsody

Rhapsody is the product of RealNetworks, Inc., a Seattle-based company which is also responsible for the RealPlayer software and the RealPlayer Music Store.

Rhapsody Summary

Pros

- Easy to use online jukebox service, with a clean, uncomplicated interface
- Big catalog of major label and independent label music
- Unlimited streaming access to catalog for a flat monthly rate
- Excellent for music discovery; critical recommendations are provided
- CD burning feature supplies portable tracks more cheaply than other major label download stores. ($0.79 instead of $0.99)

Cons

- Skimpy artist and record information
- Available only for Windows PC users
- Inability to download tracks direct to your computer

Best for

- People looking for a robust, easy-to-use online jukebox service
- People who place high importance on new music discovery
- People in a position to listen to music while connected to the Internet

10

Downloading Services
Building Your Digital Music Collection

While online jukeboxes let you rent music, downloading services let you buy it. Downloading services work by allowing you to transfer music files to your computer, after which they can be played, burned to CD, or transferred to a portable music player. Once in your possession, these files become part of your digital music collection.

Compared to a shelf-full of CDs, a digital music collection has many advantages. It takes up less space. It allows you create and share personal music mixes. And it makes it easier to browse your collection and cue up music. The better downloading services make it easy to add to your collection, and are preferable to the alternative: buying CDs, fighting with the packaging, and then copying or "ripping" the files from your CDs to your hard drive. Other reasons for using a downloading service include:

- **Near-instant delivery of music**
  Downloading services let you get the music immediately, right when you're thinking about it. There is no need to go to the music store or wait for a CD to come in the mail.

- **You have the option of buying individual songs not just albums**
  Music fans have griped for years about having to pay for a CD only to get a few songs they liked. This saves money if all you want is a song or two.

- **You own or would like to own a portable music player**
  By allowing you to take your music collection on the road, a portable music player gives you a reason for building a digital music collection.

- **You get access to material not available on CD**
  Downloading services now offer outtakes, special mixes, and performances not available on CD. The space and cost constraints involved in CD distribution don't exist online, so it is easier for the record labels to make these additional materials available.

Compared to buying CDs, using downloading services has one main drawback: the music selection—though rapidly improving—is not as good. In some cases you will need to the buy the CD and rip the files in order to add them to your digital music collection. Also, thanks to the development of a robust used CD market on sites like Amazon.com, you can sometimes buy a used CD for less money than it costs to buy the album from a downloading service.

At present, legitimate downloading services fall into three categories:

- **Download Stores**

  These services sell downloads a la carte: you pay individually for each downloaded song or album. No subscription fee is required. These services are the most numerous, and include Apple's iTunes Music Store, the RealPlayer Music Store, and Walmart Music Downloads.

- **Full Featured Music Services**

  Like the download stores, these services sell portable downloads a la carte, but also provide subscription-based online jukebox and Internet radio offerings. They include Napster and Musicmatch.

- **Subscription Based Downloading Services**

  Here, you pay a monthly fee and are allowed to download a set number of songs per month. eMusic offers such a service. Also, some services provide unlimited "tethered downloads" on a subscription basis. See the sidebar on the next page, *The Tethered Download,* for more information.

Napster and Its Offspring: The "Free" File Trading Services

You can't discuss music downloading without talking about the file trading services. These popular yet controversial services make it easy for people to exchange music files using the Internet, usually in violation of copyright law. These include the original Napster service, shut down through legal action, and its successors: Kazaa, eDonkey, and others. Though these services are free, and often have a good selection of music, they have drawbacks when compared with legitimate services:

- Downloaded files can be corrupt, incomplete, or virus-laden
- File delivery times are unpredictable, ranging from seconds to days
- There is little information to help you decide what to download
- File trading software comes with annoying pop-up ads and spyware
- Artists don't get paid
- You might get sued for copyright infringement

Choosing a Downloading Service

First, consider where you are starting from:

- **What kind of computer do you have?**
  Some services rely on jukebox software that will run only on Windows
  PCs. Others will run only on the most recent versions of the Windows or
  Macintosh operating systems. Others have a web-based interface and so
  will work with a greater range of computers (including Linux machines).

- **Do you own a portable music player?**
  Or are you considering buying one? Because different downloading
  services use different file formats, you need to make sure that your service
  uses a format that your chosen portable music player can read. For
  example, the iTunes Music Store is the only major label downloading
  service that works with Apple's iPod portable music player.

- **Are you already using a music jukebox software package?**
  If you like a particular music jukebox software package, consider using a
  service that is designed to work with it. If you like the *iTunes* jukebox
  software, then use the iTunes Music Store. If you like the *Musicmatch
  Jukebox* software, then use the Musicmatch Downloads service.

The Tethered Download

A tethered download is a music file that can only be played on your
computer. It can't be burned to CD or transferred to a portable music
player. It is tethered because you don't own it; you rent it from the music
service. Periodically the files "phone home" to see if your subscription is
current; if it isn't, they shut down and become lifeless bits taking up
space on your hard drive. Offered by some online jukebox services,
Napster most notably, tethered downloads are a means to combine the
all-you-can-drink abundance of the online jukebox—unlimited downloads
are allowed—with the ability to play the music offline. Unfortunately, tethered downloads also combine the worst of both worlds: the hassle of
managing downloads with the limited portability of the online jukebox.
This may change, however. Music services are working on offerings to
allow tethered downloads to be loaded into portable music players, in
effect allowing you to rent a portable jukebox of music.

Next, consider these factors:

- **Ease of Use**
  How easy is it to find the music you are looking for? How easy is it to download music and add it to your digital music collection? How is the customer support?

- **Selection**
  How large is the catalog? Is it strong in the genres that you care about? Does the service have exclusive material? Services with strong selections of major label software include Napster, the iTunes Music Store and Rhapsody. eMusic has a big catalog of independent label music.

- **Price**
  How much do songs and albums cost? Most download stores sell downloads for $0.99 per song. Rhapsody sells the same tracks for $0.79 a track, but their service will only let you burn tracks to CD. eMusic sells music from independent labels for $0.25 a track on a subscription basis ($9.99 per month for 40 tracks).

- **Audio file format and DRM scheme**
  Will the service's file format and the digital rights management (DRM) scheme (if any) work with the jukebox software and portable music player that you wish to use? For more information, see the sidebar on the following page, *Battling DRM Formats.*

- **Encoding Bit Rate**
  Services differ in the bit rate at which they encode their music files. For a given file format, a higher bit rate results in better sound quality and a bigger file. This is something audiophiles care about. For most people, the differences between the services will not be significant.

- **Usage restrictions**
  Most services use digital rights management (DRM) technology to restrict what you can do with their music files. This includes restricting the number of computers you can play a file on, and the number of times you can burn a file to CD or transfer it to a portable music player. With the exception of eMusic, which places no such restrictions on their files, the differences between the services are not all that significant. They key question here is: how much of a hassle is it to exercise your usage rights? If you have a problem, will customer service quickly fix it for you?

The following chapters discuss the iTunes Music Store, eMusic, and Musicmatch, all of which offer recommended downloading services. Musicmatch, in a bid to provide an all-in-one music solution, also offers Internet radio and online jukebox services.

Battling DRM Formats: Apple vs. Microsoft (and now RealNetworks)

Two digital rights management (DRM) schemes, each tied to a different audio file format, are battling for supremacy in the world of major label music downloading services. In one corner is Apple Computer, whose iTunes Music Store is selling AAC (Advanced Audio Coding) encoded files protected by an Apple proprietary DRM scheme. In the other corner are downloading services which sell WMA (Windows Media Audio) encoded files protected by a different, Microsoft DRM scheme. Portable music players and jukebox software tend to support one scheme or the other, but not both.

The most popular portable music player, Apple's iPod, supports the Apple scheme. Just about every other player supports the Microsoft scheme. Until this compatibility impasse is resolved, consumers will need to choose a service based on the format that works best with their chosen computer, portable music player, and music jukebox software. But hope may be around the corner.

As this book was going to press, RealNetworks entered the fray, announcing a DRM translation technology called Harmony, which makes downloads from its download store (which uses a third, incompatible DRM scheme) playable on portable music players using either the Apple or the Microsoft scheme. In response, Apple has cried foul, claiming that RealNetworks has "hacked" their proprietary technology. More to the point, this act threatens the iTunes Music Store's status as the only major label download store that will work with the iPod player. Apple may yet try to block this technology: stay tuned.

Note: All portable music players and music jukebox software support the older MP3 audio standard, which is free from the DRM restrictions being imposed by the major label downloading services. One way around these restrictions is to burn a CD and then rip the files using the MP3 format. This way the files can be played on your music player of choice. Another way to avoid these hassles is to buy your music from independent label oriented services like eMusic and Audio Lunchbox, who place no such restrictions on their files.

11

iTunes Music Store
Downloads for the iPod People

Apple's iTunes Music Store caused a sensation when it launched in 2003. It's early success showed that large numbers of people were willing to buy downloads online. Like other downloading services, the iTunes Music Store allows you to buy songs from a large catalog of major label and independent music for $0.99 each. It requires the use of Apple's free *iTunes* music jukebox software, now available to Windows XP and Windows 2000 users, as well as to Macintosh users. The *iTunes* software is well designed and simple to use, allowing you to download music, burn CDs, and transfer files to and from Apple's popular iPod portable music player.

The iTunes Music Store downloads are encoded using the AAC (advanced audio coding) format, and protected using Apple's FairPlay digital rights management scheme, which limits the number of computers you can play the music on (five), and the number of times that a single playlist can be burned to CD (seven). Unfortunately, few portable music players outside of the iPod will play these songs. Luckily for *iTunes* users, the iPod is considered by many to be the most desirable portable music player. To learn more about the differences between Apple's AAC files and the WMA files being sold by most other download stores, see the sidebar, *Battling DRM Formats*, on page 60.

The Catalog

Apple's music catalog is large, with over 1,000,000 tracks, and contains music from the Big 5 music labels as well as over 600 independent labels. Unique among the music services is their selection of audio-books (over 5,000) and spoken word recordings, made available by agreement with Audible.com. This includes archived shows from National Public Radio, such as *Car Talk*, *This American Life*, and *Fresh Air*. For the iPod user on the go, the availability of this material is a major plus. *Note:* Many archived National Public Radio shows can be played for free on the Web, but they require that you be connected via the Internet to listen. In addition, Apple recently got access to the Disney catalog of recordings.

Figure 11.1. *iTunes* player and jukebox

Music Discovery With iTunes

The iTunes Music Store offers music recommendations, historical Billboard charts, and celebrity created playlists with commentary. iTunes Music Store staff have also created thematic playlists (e.g., "breakup songs", "choral gems") under the heading "iTunes Essentials." The artist information includes artist biographies and album notes. More recently, Apple debuted a new feature called iMix, which allows users to create and share playlists. Also new is a collection of radio airplay charts, organized by city and by station across the U.S. For example, if you live in Wichita you can browse charts from eight different radio stations that serve that market.

The *iTunes* software also lets you listen to Internet radio stations that use the MP3 audio format. A directory of these stations is available within the player. Other MP3 radio stations can be found using the Shoutcast (http://shoutcast.com) and Live365 (http://www.live365.com/index.live) directories. iTunes Music Store customers looking for a robust Internet radio service are recommended to try Live365 (see Chapter 2). In addition to being an excellent service, its stations can be played using the *iTunes* player. A number of Live365 stations are already listed in the *iTunes* radio directory. Also, a new Macintosh version of their *Radio365* software lets listeners use the iTunes Music Store to buy tracks they hear on Live365

More Ways to Buy

In addition to the usual credit card payment options, the iTunes Music Store offers gift-certificates, prepaid cards (available at Target stores nationwide) and a scheme which lets you set music "allowances" for your children (or perhaps yourself!). America Online (AOL) users can now sign-in using their AOL screen name and buy music using their AOL account.

Getting Started

If your computer meets the system requirements, go to the *iTunes* download page (http://www.apple.com/itunes/download) and follow the instructions for downloading and installing the free *iTunes* software.

See Chapter 31, *iTunes Music Store Discovery Plan*, for a detailed seven-day plan showing you how to get up-to-speed with the iTunes Music Store, and get the most out of its features.

System Requirements - Macintosh

- 400MHz G3 processor or better
- 128 MB RAM minimum/256 RAM recommended
- Mac OS X v10.1.5 or later
- Mac OS X v10.2.4 required to share music and burn DVDs
- QuickTime 6.2 required to encode AAC

System Requirements - Windows PCs

- Windows XP or 2000
- 500 MHz Pentium class processor or better
- 128 MB RAM minimum/256 RAM recommended
- Latest Windows service packs recommended
- Supported CD-RW drive to burn CDs, video display card, soundcard
- QuickTime 6.5 (included)

Once *iTunes* is installed, start it up and click on the MUSIC STORE icon on the left side of the player. This will call up the music store home page. Here you can browse the offerings or search for specific songs, artists or albums.

If you want to buy some music, click on the ACCOUNT SIGN IN button. A box will open up, giving you the option to CREATE NEW ACCOUNT. Here you will be asked to supply your credit card and account setup information. Once this has been completed you will be able to buy music.

Tips for Using the iTunes Music Store

- **Read the iTunes Hot Tips page** - http://www.apple.com/itunes/hottips
  Learn keyboard shortcuts and get up to speed quickly with the software.

- **Become familiar with the iTunes "Smart Playlists" feature**
  This lets you automatically generate song playlists based on criteria such as ratings, genre, and the last time the song was played. A good resource is the Web site: http://www.smartplaylists.com.

- **Check used CD prices before buying albums and songs online**
  If you're willing to wait a bit, used CDs from online stores like Amazon can sometimes be cheaper than buying the downloads online.

- **Sign-up for an Internet radio or online jukebox service**
  This gives you an opportunity to listen to entire songs or albums before you decide to buy them as portable downloads.

- **Use the Allmusic Web site to obtain more artist information**
  The Allmusic site (http://www.allmusic.com) will supply record details, ratings, reviews, and more detailed artist information. This will supplement the limited artist information provided by Apple.

Other Resources

- **iPod & iTunes: The Missing Manual, 2nd Edition**
  Published in February 2004, this is the most up-to-date book on using *iTunes* and the iPod. More information is available at the O'Reilly Publishing Web site: http://www.oreilly.com/catalog/ipodtmm2/index.html.

- **Doug's AppleScripts for iTunes** - http://www.malcolmadams.com/itunes
  For the more technically oriented, this site helps Macintosh users automate tasks and manage information using iTunes. Free AppleScripts are made available.

- **iPodlounge** - http://www.ipodlounge.com
  "All things iPod" is the slogan for this Web site, which serves as an online community for iPod owners. It provides news, articles, product reviews, and online forums where registered users can exchange information about iPods and related software and accessories.

- **Yahoo Group for iPod Users** - http://groups.yahoo.com/group/AppleiPod
  This online forum allows you to ask questions of iPod owners and enthusiasts. You can also search for answers to questions in the message archive.

iTunes Music Store Summary

Pros

- Well designed, easy-to-use download store
- Big catalog of major label and independent label music
- No subscription is required
- Well integrated with Apple's popular iPod portable music player
- Good collection of audio-books and spoken word recordings
- Numerous payment options, including a "music allowance" feature
- Works on both Macintosh and Windows PCs

Cons

- The only portable music player supported is the iPod
- *iTunes* software won't play the Windows Media Audio (WMA) files sold by other download stores
- No online jukebox or premium Internet radio option is provided
- Other services provide cheaper downloads (eMusic, Walmart)
- No support for older operating systems (Win 98, Win ME, Mac OS9)

Best for

- iPod owners (PC and Macintosh users)
- Macintosh owners
- People looking for access to a download store only

12

eMusic
Downloading for Discovery

If you're interested in discovering new music and economically expanding your music library with downloads, then eMusic deserves a good look. A subscription-based downloading service, eMusic charges significantly less per-track than mainstream services like the iTunes Music Store. What's more, eMusic's downloads are in the MP3 format, free from the usage restrictions and digital rights management (DRM) schemes imposed by the other downloading services. This means that you can play your music on almost any portable music player, and can move your files around, hassle-free.

Because these terms are relatively generous, the major record labels and top-selling acts don't sell their music here. But over 1,200 independent record labels do, making eMusic a rich destination for music lovers. eMusic's catalog has over 500,000 tracks from over 24,000 artists, and includes rich archives of historically important music. Think of eMusic as a cross between a college town record store, where you'll find lots of underground and truly independent music, and one of those used record stores where you can find amazing old classics for next to nothing. eMusic also offers recordings of live club performances from around the country through it's eMusicLive program.

As a subscription-based service, eMusic requires you to spend a minimum of $10 a month on the service, and so is not recommended for someone who is happy buying one or two CDs per year. But for the more active buyer, eMusic represents a good value, providing subscribers an ongoing stream of reasonably priced downloads. The free trial is generous, and the subscription, which runs from month to month, can be cancelled at any time.

Getting music is a matter of browsing the eMusic Web site, and selecting individual tracks or albums to download. The downloading process is handled by the *eMusic Download Manager* (see Figure 12.1) software, versions of which are available for Windows, Macintosh, and Linux users. If you lose your files or need to download them to another computer, eMusic will let you download them again. Provided your subscription is active, repeat downloads will not count against your monthly allocation of tracks.

Figure 12.1. eMusic Download Manager

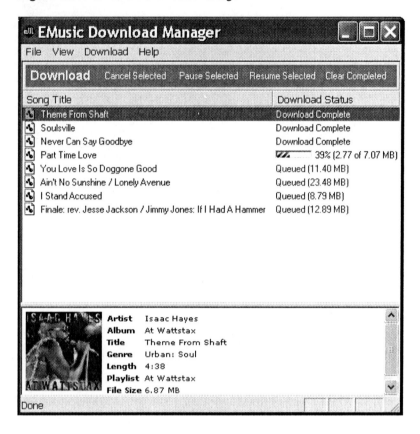

Music Discovery with eMusic

The variety of eMusic's catalog is one the service's main assets. By definition, much of the music comes from outside the commercial mainstream. Like Rhapsody, eMusic has done a good job of providing paths into the catalog. The newly redesigned Web site lets you browse music by genre and subgenre, decade and region. TOP ALBUMS (listed by popularity) and EDITOR'S PICKS lists can also be browsed. These music listings can then be further refined. For example, if you are browsing albums under the category of Jazz Fusion, you can click on the REFINE BY: TOP ALBUMS link to get a list of top albums in the subgenre of Jazz Fusion. Clicking on the REFINE BY: EDITOR'S PICKS link will now restrict this list to albums that are also EDITOR'S PICKS. Clicking on additional REFINE BY links will filter the list further. eMusic lets you search for music by artist, album, or track name—like most other services—but also lets you search by composer or record label.

Other tools are available to help you choose what to download. Album reviews and artist biographies are supplied from the makers of the Allmusic Web site. Columns and essays from leading music journalists, in which eMusic offerings are discussed, are also supplied. Thirty second music samples let you listen before you download. When you find albums of interest, you can bookmark them by clicking on a link marked, SAVE FOR LATER.

The CHARTS button at the top of the home page takes you to various Top 20 chart lists. These include lists of the Top 20 most popular songs, artists, albums, record labels, and live performances (taken from the eMusicLive program). As new artists or recordings come into the mix, the charts change. A scan of top artists will reveal any big-name artists whose material was recently included. Optional e-mail newsletters will alert you to new releases in your genres of interest.

Community Features

eMusic's message boards allow you to discuss music with other eMusic subscribers and see what they are listening to and recommending. There are message boards for each of the major categories of music (e.g., electronic, rock/pop, jazz, classical) as well as a general message board for discussions that aren't specific to a particular genre of music. You can also create and save lists of favorite albums and songs, add your personal commentary, and then share them with other subscribers. Or, if you choose, keep them private.

Effective September 2004, subscribers can post reviews and ratings of albums, and view the music preferences of other subscribers. These include NEIGHBORS and FRIENDS. NEIGHBORS are subscribers who exhibit similar downloading patterns to your own. FRIENDS are subscribers whose music profiles you have chosen to keep tabs on.

Your eMusic Profile

Reachable from the toolbar at the top of every page, the YOUR PROFILE page is where you can access your personal eMusic information. Here you can access a list of tracks and albums you have downloaded, your SAVE FOR LATER list, your ratings and reviews, as well as any other lists that you may have created. Here you can also access the profiles of your eMusic NEIGHBORS and FRIENDS.

The EDIT PROFILE button gives you the option of making your personal information visible to other subscribers, including your name, location, gender, e-mail address, and Yahoo IM handle. You can also post an ABOUT ME statement up to 250 words long.

The Catalog

In addition to lots of new music from independent music labels, there are lots of records from historically significant artists—jazz artists and blues artists in particular. Listed below is a sampling of artists from the catalog. You are encouraged to browse the listings on the eMusic Web site. As of September 27, 2004, there were 49,087 albums available from 1,224 record labels.

Rock/Pop
Creedence Clearwater Revival
The Kinks
Van Morrison
Violent Femmes

Country/Folk
The Carter Family
Johnny Cash
Merle Haggard
Willie Nelson

Jazz
John Coltrane
Ella Fitzgerald
Benny Goodman
Thelonious Monk

Blues
R. L. Burnside
Lightning Hopkins
John Lee Hooker
B.B. King

Electronic
Boards of Canada
The Future Sound of London
Prodigy
Thievery Corporation

Classical
Beethoven
Mozart
Wagner
Haydn

Urban/Hip Hop
Blackalicious
James Brown
Otis Redding
Public Enemy

New Age
Basque
Suzanne Ciani
Michael Allen Harrison
Steven Halpern

World/Reggae
Bob Marley And The Wailers
The Fenians
R. Carlos Nakai
Steeleye Span

Inspirational
Sam Cooke
Dottie Peoples
The Staple Singers
Soul Stirrers

Alternative/Punk
Belle and Sebastian
Pavement
Tom Waits
Yo La Tengo

Soundtracks/Other
Lenny Bruce
George Carlin
Noam Chomsky
Ennio Morricone

Access Options

- **Free trial**
  eMusic offers a 14-day free trial and the ability to download 50 tracks before having to buy a subscription.

- **eMusic Basic**
  This subscription plan allows you to download 40 tracks per month for $9.99 per month.

- **eMusic Plus / Premium**
  eMusic Plus allows you to download 65 tracks per month for $14.99 per month. eMusic Premium allows you to download 90 tracks per month for $19.99 per month.

These subscription plans run month to month and can be cancelled at any time. Unfortunately, any unused tracks are *not* carried over to the next month. Additional tracks, that *do* carry over, can be purchased in the form of "booster packs." A 10 track booster pack costs $4.99 (50 cents per track); a 25 track pack costs $9.99 (40 cents per track); a 50 track pack costs $14.99 (30 cents per track). These options can be managed from your eMusic ACCOUNT page.

Getting Started

First, make sure you have jukebox software installed on your computer that will let you store, organize, and play MP3 files. Options include *Musicmatch Jukebox*, *Media Jukebox* and Apple's *iTunes* jukebox software.

Next, go to the eMusic Web site (http://www.emusic.com) and sign-up for the free trial-subscription that is offered. Then, follow instructions for downloading the version of the *eMusic Download Manager* software that is appropriate for your computer operating system. Supported operating systems include Windows 98/ME/2000/XP, Macintosh OS 9/10, and Linux). Now start downloading and playing some music!

See Chapter 32, *eMusic Discovery Plan*, for a detailed seven-day plan showing you how to get up-to-speed with eMusic, and get the most out of it.

Tips for Using eMusic

- **Look for recommendations from other subscribers**
  Use the message boards to find album recommendations and commentary posted by other eMusic subscribers. Lists posted by other subscribers can also be a good source of recommendations.

- **Use the album reviews to help you decide what to download**
  Some of these albums haven't made it big commercially for good reason. Use the Allmusic supplied reviews when they are available. If necessary, go elsewhere to find a review. See Chapter 18, *Finding Album Reviews*, for more information.

- **Use the CHARTS and NEW ARRIVALS pages to scan for new albums**
  The popularity charts on eMusic are fairly dynamic. Interesting new albums shoot to the top with regularity.

- **Use the SAVE FOR LATER feature to bookmark albums**
  This is helpful when you find an interesting album, but aren't ready to download it yet.

- **Make sure you have enough disk space**
  Downloading from eMusic will fill up your hard disk at a rate of one megabyte (MB) per minute of music. So if you plan to use the service, I recommend allocating at least five gigabytes (GB) of disk space. If you're pinched for space, remember that you can delete albums and re-download them later, provided your account remains active.

eMusic Pitfalls

- **Downloads that don't carry over from month to month**
  Each monthly allocation of downloads expires at the end the month. If
  you don't use them, you lose them. I like to download albums rather than
  individual songs, which means I'm inevitably left with three or four
  unused downloads at the end of the month and no convenient way to use
  them. The newly available "booster pack" downloads, which cost more
  and do not expire, help to address this problem. But they make using the
  service that much more complicated.

- **Inconsistent Track Tags**
  Some albums contain MP3 information tags that are inconsistent from
  track to track. For example, there might be slight variations in the album
  name that cause songs to appear as though they are on two separate
  albums. Jukebox software software can be used to edit the track tags and
  correct this problem.

About eMusic

Founded in 1998, eMusic became the first commercial site to begin selling
singles and albums in the MP3 format. In the fall of 2000, eMusic became the
first company to launch a downloadable music subscription service. eMusic
was acquired by Dimensional Associates LLC, a private investment firm, in
the fall of 2003.

eMusic Summary

Pros

- Best selection of independent label music—great for music discovery
- Good selection of music from historically important artists
- Cost per track is 25 cents or less
- MP3 files can be played on most portable music players, including the iPod
- MP3 files are free of digital rights management (DRM) restrictions & hassles
- Rich music information including reviews, artist information, and articles
- Ability of subscribers to share discoveries through message boards and "favorites" lists
- Available to Windows, Macintosh, and Linux users

Cons

- Major label artists and music are largely absent
- "Use them or lose them" expiring downloads
- No online jukebox or premium Internet radio option is provided

Best for

- People looking to build a portable music library economically
- People interested in alternatives to mainstream commercial music
- People who prefer their music files free of digital rights management (DRM)
- Active music buyers

13

Musicmatch Online
One Stop Shop for Digital Music

Musicmatch is best known for its *Musicmatch Jukebox* software, which allows Windows PC owners to play music, manage their digital music collections, and burn CDs. More recently, they have developed a suite of online music services that can be accessed using *Musicmatch Jukebox*. This includes Musicmatch Radio, available in free and fee-based versions; Musicmatch Downloads, an a la carte download store; and Musicmatch On-Demand, a subscription-based online jukebox service. Thus, *Musicmatch Jukebox* is no longer just a tool for managing your digital music files. It's a one-stop digital music store too.

Musicmatch Jukebox makes it easy to switch between listening to radio and playing tracks on-demand, and between playback of locally stored tracks and streaming tracks stored on Musicmatch's servers: both kinds of tracks can be combined in a single playlist. Add seamless access to rich music information and you get a veritable Swiss Army knife for the digital music explorer. What's more, Musicmatch has put these features into an easy-to-use package.

The software required to use these services, *Musicmatch Jukebox*, comes in a free, basic version and a "Plus" version, currently priced at $19.95 (plus $39.95 for access to "all future upgrades"). The free version is fine for starting out, and can be used to access all of Musicmatch's services. But if you are serious about managing a collection of digital music files, I recommend upgrading to the Plus version, which has more features and lets you rip and burn CDs more quickly. *Musicmatch Jukebox* is regarded as a "best-of-breed" jukebox package for Windows users, and has won PC Magazine's "editor's pick" designation five times in a row. Unlike the competing *iTunes* jukebox software, it works with older versions of Windows (Windows 98 and Windows ME).

When it comes to DRM-protected music downloads, Musicmatch supports Microsoft's standard and not Apple's (see sidebar "Battling DRM Formats" on page 60). This means that downloads purchased from Musicmatch won't work with Apple's iPod portable players. They will play, however, in portable music players from a range of other manufacturers, including Rio, Creative, Diamond, Phillips, and Hewlett-Packard.

Musicmatch Radio

Musicmatch provides three Internet radio options:

- **Musicmatch Radio**
  This free, ad-supported offering provides over 200 stations, streamed at a low bit rate. Available worldwide.

- **Premium Musicmatch Radio - Gold**
  This provides everything the free service has, but is ad-free and provides "CD quality" music streams. It also provides the ability to play "Era" stations, which play music from a specific year or decade, and "Artist Match" stations, which play music by your selected artist and related artists. The subscription costs $2.95 per month, billed annually (or $4.95 per month, billed monthly). Available worldwide.

- **Premium Musicmatch Radio - Platinum**
  For $4.95 per month, billed annually (or $6.95 per month, billed monthly), this subscription plan provides everything that Premium Radio Gold does, but adds the ability to play "Artist Stations", which play *only* music by your selected artists. For licensing reasons, this option is only available in the U.S. and Canada.

Figure 13.1. *Musicmatch Jukebox* playing West Coast Jazz radio station

All radio users can pause or skip tracks, and can use the NOW PLAYING button to get information about the track being played. The CD QUALITY button lets you toggle between two sound quality settings: CD and LOW. The LOW quality setting is used when your Internet connection is slow.

Musicmatch Jukebox can also use the active playlist to generate a custom radio station. It does this by harvesting artist names from the playlist and creating an Artist Match station on the fly. If a track is available for purchase through the Musicmatch Downloads service, a BUY TRACK button will appear next to the track name. Seven-day free trials are available for all of Musicmatch's subscription services.

Figure 13.2. Musicmatch Artist Radio page for Frank Sinatra

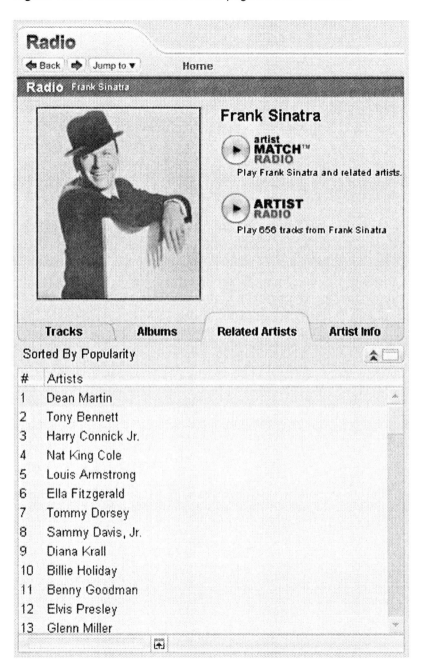

Musicmatch On-Demand

Musicmatch's highest tier subscription service is Musicmatch On-Demand, an online jukebox service that lets you play any or all of the tracks in Musicmatch's streaming catalog (600,000+ tracks), and which includes access to all of Musicmatch's premium radio services. At present this catalog is smaller than Rhapsody's, but I expect this difference to become less significant over time. The catalog can be browsed by genre, era, and artist. Within these categories, tracks and artists are displayed in order of popularity with Musicmatch users. The catalog can also be searched by track, album, or artist. On the genre pages no attempt is made, as with the Rhapsody service, to highlight important albums or artists from a critical perspective, or to draw attention to such albums and artists when they are not available in their catalog.

Albums and tracks from Musicmatch's streaming catalog can be "saved" to your *Musicmatch Jukebox* library even though the tracks themselves are stored on Musicmatch's servers. Within the library display, a streaming icon appears next to streaming tracks so as to differentiate them from the portable tracks stored on your computer. These streaming tracks can be included in your *Musicmatch Jukebox* playlists. They cannot, however, be played unless you are connected to the Internet. Neither can they be burned to CD. To do this, you need to buy and download the tracks using the Musicmatch Downloads service. *Musicmatch Jukebox* also has an explicit lyrics filter setting that can be used to block profanity when using Musicmatch Radio or Musicmatch On-Demand.

On a month-to-month basis, Musicmatch On-Demand costs the same as Rhapsody, $9.95 per month. But if you are willing to prepay for longer periods of time, the cost is less: $8.95 per month, billed quarterly; and $7.95 per month, billed annually.

Musicmatch Downloads

Music discovered while listening to Musicmatch's radio and on-demand services can be purchased, and made portable, for $0.99 a track. Musicmatch Downloads is a pay-as-you-go download store accessible within *Musicmatch Jukebox*. Tracks are delivered in the WMA format, with DRM imposed restrictions, and are encoded at a bit rate of 160 Kbps, compared to 128 Kbps for tracks from Napster and other WMA-based downloading services. These tracks can be played on up to five computers, transferred to portable music players (but not the iPod), and burned to CD up to five times per playlist. Music can be purchased by credit card or gift certificate. There is also an allowance feature that lets parents give access to their children while limiting the amount that can be spent per month.

Music Discovery with Musicmatch

Musicmatch is one of the best services when it comes to providing tools for music discovery. First there is Musicmatch Radio, with its large number of artist, era, and genre specific stations, and a wealth of paths of follow. Then there is music information on tap: click on the NOW PLAYING button and you'll be served an Allmusic guide page for the song and album being played. From here, you can follow links to additional artist and genre information, and receive recommendations of other artists to try.

If you don't have time to pursue an interesting track or album, bookmark it using Musicmatch's MY WISHLIST feature. You'll then be able to return later to research it, play it, or buy it. Being able to play full albums without having to buy them is a further boon to music exploration, and Musicmatch's On-Demand service lets you do that to your heart's content. You also have the option of receiving personalized music recommendations. This requires that you list your top ten favorite artists and agree to let Musicmatch upload your play logs.

Musicmatch has lagged other services when it comes to providing community features that let subscribers discuss music and share recommendations. Unlike Napster and eMusic, Musicmatch doesn't provide message boards for users to share music recommendations. Neither does it provide a forum for posting music mixes, as does the iTunes Music Store. It does, however, let you e-mail your streaming playlists to your friends, allowing them to play the first twenty tracks of each playlist up to three times (using *Musicmatch Jukebox*)—even if they aren't subscribers. Rhapsody offers a similar feature, but the recipients have to be subscribers to play the tracks.

Getting Started

Download the *Musicmatch Jukebox* software (http://www.musicmatch.com) and sign-up for the Musicmatch On-Demand free trial. During the software installation, you will be prompted on whether you want to "opt-in" to personalization. If you do, you are consenting to have your play logs uploaded and used by Musicmatch for their music recommendations process. See Chapter 33, *Musicmatch Online Discovery Plan*, for a detailed seven-day plan showing you how to get up-to-speed with Musicmatch's Online services.

System Requirements

- Windows 98/ME/NT/2000/XP and Internet Explorer 6.0 or later
- Pentium Class 300MHz processor or better
- 128 MB RAM / 250 MB hard drive space (500 MB recommended for radio)
- SoundBlaster compatible sound card

Tips for using Musicmatch Online

- **Use the MY WISHLIST and NOW PLAYING features**
  Adding a song to your Musicmatch wishlist is a great way of bookmarking songs for future reference, while the NOW PLAYING link allows you to read about music and artists while you listen—a very useful feature!

- **Use ARTIST MATCH and ARTIST RADIO stations differently**
  Artist Radio stations are best for focusing on an artist's work, while Artist Match stations are best for discovering music by related artists, as determined by the listening tastes of other *Musicmatch Jukebox* users.

- **Explore the full range of genre specific radio stations**
  Clicking on each genre category in the STATIONS menu won't reveal all the genre stations available to you. Under each genre category there is link to a page listing *all* the stations for that category (e.g., ALL JAZZ STYLES). Click on this link to get the full listing. When I last checked there were 20 Blues styles and 108 Rock/Pop styles to choose from.

- **Use Era Stations to revisit periods of your life**
  Do you want to hear the music that was playing the year you were born? Music that played while you were in school? The year you got married? Then try the Era stations. Era stations can also be used to find artists that are associated with a particular year or decade, from 1960 on.

- **Use *Musicmatch Jukebox* to manage your digital music files**
  If you have music files that need to be managed and aren't wedded to another Jukebox offering, take the time to learn the ins and outs of the *Musicmatch Jukebox* software. It will be worth your while, even if you don't end up using Musicmatch's subscription services.

- **Listen before buying music downloads**
  While this may seem obvious, it's worth listening to a track a few times before spending $0.99 to buy it. Your $0.99 is making the song portable. Ask yourself: do I really need to make this song portable? A Musicmatch On-Demand subscription is required to be able to do this.

- **Check used CD prices before buying an album**
  If you're willing to wait a bit, and don't mind "ripping" the files using *Musicmatch Jukebox*, used CDs from online stores like Amazon.com can sometimes be cheaper than downloading the album from Musicmatch.

Musicmatch Pitfalls

- **Musicmatch Upgrade causes you to lose Jukebox Plus**
  Each time there is a significant *Musicmatch Jukebox* upgrade, you are
  encouraged to download the new version. If you buy *Musicmatch Jukebox
  Plus*, but don't opt to buy "All Future Upgrades" (which costs $39.99
  extra), installing the new version will result in losing your "Plus" features.
  If you then decide, as I did, that you want to buy "All Future Upgrades",
  you will have to pay for the Jukebox software *again*, in addition to the
  "All Future Upgrades" fee. To avoid this irritation, I suggest not opting for
  Musicmatch Jukebox Plus unless you are willing to part with the money
  for "All Future Upgrades." Alternately, you can refuse to install future
  upgrades, and in this way, maintain access to your "Plus" features.

About Musicmatch

Founded in 1997, Musicmatch produces the *Musicmatch Jukebox* software,
which allows Windows users to play, rip, burn, and organize their music. Musicmatch also produces the Musicmatch Radio, Musicmatch Downloads, and
Musicmatch On-Demand services. There are over 55 million registered copies
of Musicmatch Jukebox and over 200,000 subscribers to their online services.
Based in San Diego, Musicmatch is a privately held company.

Musicmatch Online Summary

Pros

- Provides an all-in-one music solution: Internet radio, online jukebox, and downloading service
- Provides "best-in-breed" jukebox software for managing your digital music collection
- Instant access to rich music information from the Allmusic guide
- Ability to share on-demand playlists with non-subscribers
- Discounted pricing for longer commitment subscriptions
- Platinum Radio provides a low-cost, "near on-demand" alternative to an online jukebox subscription
- Works with older versions of Windows (Win 98/ Win ME)

Cons

- All-in-one solution may be too complicated for some people
- *Musicmatch Jukebox Plus* is aggressively marketed and costs extra; installed upgrades will nullify your "Plus" status unless you buy "All Future Upgrades"
- Downloads won't work with Apple's iPod portable music players
- Only works with Windows PCs

Best for

- Windows PC owners looking for an all-in-one digital music service
- People who place high importance on new music discovery
- People in a position to listen to music while connected to the Internet
- Existing *Musicmatch Jukebox* users

14

Napster
& Other On-Demand Services

Beyond the services profiled thus far, there are other on-demand services that deserve attention. These include Napster, Streamwaves, Audio Lunchbox, and Walmart's download store. With the exception of Napster and Audio Lunchbox, the services covered in this chapter are only available in the U.S.

Napster - http://www.napster.com

Launched in October 2003, Napster 2.0 bears the name of the file trading service that kick-started the music downloading revolution. And while it doesn't allow file sharing like the original Napster, it is as full-featured and ambitious as any service. Napster 2.0 has it all: a big music catalog, an a la carte download store, and a subscription offering that features ad-free Internet radio, an online jukebox, and tethered downloads that can be played offline.

Its music discovery features are equally comprehensive. In addition to the Internet radio and online jukebox options, it provides rich artist and album information from the Allmusic guide as well as historical Billboard charts. Also provided are Napster popularity charts, an online music magazine, and editor created playlists. Available music can be browsed by genre and subgenre or searched by artist, album, or track. Newly added music can be browsed by genre as well.

Napster's community features also foster music discovery. Subscribers can share playlists, browse each other's Napster music collections, and see what music other subscribers are "now streaming" at a given moment. They can send one another messages and participate in genre specific message boards.

All these features come with a price: complexity. Because the Napster software is a plug-in to Microsoft's *Windows Media Player* jukebox software, these many features are shoehorned into one window, outside of which lie buttons that have nothing to do with using Napster. The result: a cluttered interface that makes Napster harder to use than other services. For those who use *Windows Media Player* as their primary jukebox software, this may be an acceptable tradeoff, given the rich functionality that Napster provides.

Downloaded files are delivered using Microsoft's WMA format, encoded at 128 Kbps, and can be played on up to three computers. These files fall into two categories: "purchased tracks" and "downloads." Napster "downloads" are, in effect, tethered downloads: they cannot be burned to CD or transferred to a portable music player. However, you can download as many of them as you like, provided you are a Napster Premium subscriber. Purchased tracks can be burned to CD or transferred to a range of portable music players, including a Napster branded player made by Samsung. See the Napster Web site for a list of compatible players (http://www.napster.com/compatible_devices). Not included on this list are Apple's popular iPod players, which support the competing AAC file format and are protected with Apple's proprietary digital rights management (DRM) scheme. For more on this issue, see the sidebar on page 60, *Battling DRM Formats*.

Portable downloads are sold by the track at $0.99, while the subscription offering, Napster Premium, costs $9.95 per month. Napster also sells prepaid "Track Packs" online which allow customers to buy tracks in bulk at discounted rates (e.g., 50 tracks for $39.95, which works out to $0.80 per track). Prepaid music cards available from major retailers (e.g., Best Buy, ExxonMobil, Riteaid) make it possible to buy downloads without a credit card. This is a good feature for kids. For parents, there is an option to filter out music with explicit lyrics.

The Internet radio service includes 45+ ad-free stations and the ability to skip tracks. Unique to Napster is the ability to see the station playlist, including tracks not yet played, and to jump around in the playlist. A personalized radio feature lets you create a station by using your Napster music collection, either by selecting a group of tracks or by using your entire collection as the basis of the station. One problem with their radio offering: you can't see the name of the song currently playing without clicking on a separate "now playing" button. With other services, this information is always visible.

The online jukebox provides on-demand access to most of the catalog (some music can only be purchased). Music played via the online jukebox is of lower fidelity than the downloaded files, 96 Kbps rather than 128 Kbps. Playlists can be created and saved, and can include both online jukebox (streaming) selections and downloads. One plus: it's easy to add tracks to any of your saved playlists. One minus: the active playlist cannot be edited. You can add to it but you can't change the order or delete songs while you are listening to it.

A Windows PC running either Windows XP or Windows 2000 is required to use Napster. Also required is *Internet Explorer* 5.01 or higher, and *Windows Media Player* 7.1 or higher. As of May 2004, a version of the Napster service is available in the U.K. A Canadian version is slated for rollout later in 2004.

Streamwaves - http://www.streamwaves.com

This online jukebox service requires no specialized software, so it's available to Macintosh OS X users as well as Windows users. Current versions of *Internet Explorer* and *Windows Media Player* are required to use it. This is the only significant online jukebox service available to Macintosh users. Its catalog is sizeable (450,000+ songs) and its interface is clean and useful, making it easy to navigate through the available music and to search for artists, albums, and songs. Playlists can then be created and saved. A small number of ad-free radio stations are also provided. A no-commitment subscription costs $9.99 per month. The price drops to $8.99 per month if you subscribe on quarterly basis, and to $7.99 per month on an annual basis. A free trial is available. This service is best for Macintosh OS X users looking for an online jukebox solution.

Audio Lunchbox - http://audiolunchbox.com

Like eMusic, Audio Lunchbox provides unrestricted, DRM-free MP3 downloads from independent label artists. Its per track prices are higher, but unlike eMusic, it requires no subscription to use. In addition, it also provides buyers with the option of receiving files in the Ogg Vorbis open source audio format. Cover art, and in some cases, album notes and lyrics are also provided. It's catalog is small (100,000 tracks and 200 labels) but growing. At present, artist information and reviews are limited. Tracks can be purchased with major credit cards or Pay Pal, and free tracks are available with the purchase of pre-paid "Lunch Cards." Audio Lunchbox uses a Web interface, making it available to the broadest range of computer users, including Macintosh, Linux, and Windows users. This service is a welcome addition for independent music lovers who want their music free of DRM restrictions and playable on the widest number of portable music players. Audio Lunchbox is available worldwide.

RealPlayer Music store - http://www.real.com/musicstore

Launched in January 2004, this download store is designed for users of RealNetwork's new *RealPlayer 10* jukebox software. Although *RealPlayer 10* has the distinction of being able play more different file formats than any other jukebox player, it is marred by a tendency to aggressively push product offers into the faces of its users. Similar to many other download stores in price and selection, this service is distinguished by its use of high-fidelity, 196 Kbps encoded AAC files, the same format used by Apple's iTunes service (Apple's files are encoded at 128 Kbps), but protected by a different digital rights management (DRM) scheme. Until recently, this meant that these files could not be played in the majority of portable music players. This included Apples's iPod and the many available Windows Audio (WMA) players. In July 2004, RealNetworks announced a technology called Harmony, which translates between different DRM schemes, thus making its tracks playable in most any portable music player. Whether this scheme breaks the compatibility impasse that affects portable download business remains to be seen. Apple has loudly protested this move, which threatens its near-monopoly on the major label download business, and could work to thwart it.

This issue aside, the RealPlayer Music Store is attractive and well organized, and provides numerous ways to browse the music. Reviews and other content are provided by RealNetwork's other music service, Rhapsody (discussed in Chapter 9).

Walmart Music Downloads - http://musicdownloads.walmart.com

Positioned as a low-cost download store, Walmart's newly launched service sells major label music downloads for $0.88 per track. Tracks are delivered as WMA files, encoded at 128 Kbps. They can be burned to CD up to ten times, transferred to WMA compatible portable music players, and played on one computer (with two "backup" computers allowed). Music can be browsed by genre or searched by artist, album, or song title. Brief album reviews and artist profiles are provided. The music selection is smaller than that of other download stores, but is expected to grow. If you want to buy songs with explicit lyrics, you will need to go elsewhere; here, you will only find edited versions of such songs. This service is available to Windows PC users (Win 98SE, Win ME, Win 2000, Win XP) running Internet Explorer 5.5 or greater and Windows Media Player 9.0 or greater. It is also available from within the Digital Media Mall featured in Microsoft's new Windows Media Player 10. Walmart gift cards can be used to purchase downloads. Though not as compelling as offerings from Napster, Musicmatch, and the iTunes Music Store, it is a cheaper alternative.

Musicnet@AOL

Available as a premium add-on service to America Online (AOL) subscribers, Musicnet@AOL is an online jukebox service. Like Napster, it provides access to tethered downloads. A small, fixed number of portable downloads (burnable to CD) are available by subscription. Users are sent to the iTunes Music Store to purchase a la carte downloads. The catalog is large, the price is reasonable ($8.95 /mo.), and a month-long free trial is available. Unfortunately, the player interface makes it hart to explore the music in the catalog. Users are limited to keyword searches and browsing a huge alphabetical list of artists. A separate download is required to install the dedicated player software (available for Windows PCs only). If the interface could be fixed, this service will be worth a second look for AOL users. As is, this service is not recommended.

Music Now - http://music.fullaudio.com

Available as a premium music service within Microsoft's *Windows Media Player* software, Music Now is a full-featured music service like Napster. It provides Internet radio, an online jukebox, and a downloading service. One big problem: the online jukebox component of Music Now has no playlist capability. You can choose only between playing individual tracks or albums. To have access to playlists, you need to download tracks and use the playlist feature in Windows Media Player. Free trials are available. In a separate venture with Best Buy, Music Now offers ala carte purchasing of downloads from a catalog of 400,000+ tracks (http://bestbuy.fullaudio.com). Not recommended.

BuyMusic at Buy.com - http://www.buymusic.com

BuyMusic is a Windows-based download store best known for offering downloads as cheaply as $0.79 per track. The pricing here varies, so most songs cannot be had for this price. Also, the usage restrictions vary from track to track, making for some confusion. Buying music is not as easy as it is with either the iTunes Music Store or Musicmatch Downloads. For example, in order to download an album you have select each song individually. The music discovery tools are also scant. Use of this service requires Microsoft's *Internet Explorer* 5.01 or higher, and *Windows Media Player* 9.0. Tracks are delivered as WMA files, encoded at 128 Kbps. Not recommended.

Sony Connect - http://www.connect.com

This newly launched download store delivers music in Sony's proprietary ATRAC file format and is aimed at owners of Sony portable music players (the only players to support this format). Sony Connect's catalog and pricing are comparable to other mainstream download services. One exception: it charges double for every song over seven minutes long. To use this service, you need to use Sony's SonicStage jukebox software, which has been widely panned by reviewers for its awkward interface and lack of support for the MP3 audio format. Community features and editorial content are minimal. This service is for Sony die-hards only.

Coming Soon!

As this book goes to press, Microsoft has launched a beta version of their own download store. Early reviews paint a picture of an adequate but not especially groundbreaking service. Later this year, Yahoo is expected to launch an on-demand music service to accompany their LAUNCHcast radio offering. An MTV-branded service is also in the works. For updated information, go to the Giant Path Web site at http://www.giantpath.com.

15

Free On-Demand Services

Promotional on-demand services let you download or play music in order to generate interest in an artist's music. The music is freely provided in the hope that it will stimulate music sales. Though the free content is limited—usually only a track or two from a given album—these sites should not be overlooked as tools for discovering new music. Use them to sample entire songs from an artist or to troll for interesting new music. The price is right!

Major record labels promote their music through large Web portals like Yahoo (http://launch.yahoo.com), AOL/Netscape (http://channels.netscape.com/ns/music), and MSN (http://music.msn.com). On these sites you can download and play singles from new albums; watch videos and listen to Internet radio; and read news, interviews, gossip, and trivia. If you're looking to browse free downloads from popular artists, try Artist Direct (http://listen.artistdirect.com), where you can browse available songs by genre, listed in order of popularity. Free downloads can also be had at Amazon.com, where there is a FREE DOWNLOADS section in the music store.

MP3.com and Its Successors

Other Web sites cater to smaller acts and aspiring artists who wish to promote their music. Though lacking in music by big-name artists, these sites contain a greater variety and quantity of free music, including music from less commercial genres like classical, jazz, and world music. Until recently, the foremost of these sites was MP3.com, considered the granddaddy of all digital music sites. At its height, it provided access to more than a million songs, more than any fee-based music service. The band playing at the club down the street probably had music on MP3.com. Unfortunately, the service was shut down this last December by its owner, Vivendi Universal. The Web publisher CNET bought the rights to the name, but not the music archive, and has relaunched MP3.com (http://mp3.com) as an information-only Web site. At the same time, CNET has setup an area for artists to load their music on its Download.com site (http://music.download.com). This site, however, is only a shadow of the former MP3.com, containing just 29,000 songs (as of this writing), and lacking in the reviews, ratings, and charts that MP3.com once had.

A better claimant to the mantle of successor to MP3.com is the GarageBand service (http://www.garageband.com). Not only does this site have a lot more music, 186,000 songs (as of this writing), but it contains reviews, ratings, and charts to help you sort through it. It has a radio feature which allows you to play the highest rated songs by genre, complete with links to reviews and artist information (see figure 15.1). What's more, GarageBand has negotiated to get access to most of the original MP3.com music archive. The catch is that the artists whose material used to be on MP3.com have to sign-up to get their music moved to the new site, which means it may be a while before GarageBand catalog approaches the size of the original MP3.com. RealNetwork's RealPlayer software is required to use this service.

Figure 15.1. GarageBand Radio

Another contender to fill the void left by the closure of MP3.com is Besonic (http://www.besonic.com), a German-owned site containing 80,000 tracks from over 44,000 artists and a wide range of genres. At this site, listeners can use charts, ratings, and reviews to help decide what to listen to. The charts are broken down by genre and nation, and songs can be played or downloaded. One nice feature is the ability to launch a playlist with an entire chart (top 50 tracks) into your music player. Registered users can also rate music and use message boards to communicate with the artists and with one another.

Another major site is Vitaminic (http://www.vitaminic.com), whose Italian owners assure us the site has nothing to do with vitamins. Instead, it provides a large collection of songs for downloading and streaming. Here you can find Italian ska and German hip hop on the menu, along with lots of other music from European artists.

Amid the din of artists clamoring for attention on these sites, there is the real problem of how to find the best music. Charts based on popularity are relied on heavily, though some sites—like GarageBand—use a rating process. One service, Epitonic (http://www.epitonic.com), has tackled the quality problem by featuring only music that passes the critical review of its editors. Though their catalog is much smaller than the other services discussed here, it is a great place to discover new music.

16

Looking Ahead

The next year promises to see a lot of activity in the online music space. The existing flock of services will continue to tweak their offerings and jockey for position. The selection of music will continue to grow, as more music gets licensed for online delivery, and additional services come online. Meanwhile, continued growth in broadband Internet connections will make online music increasingly accessible. San Diego just became the first American city in which the number of broadband connections exceeds the number of dial-up connections. Other cities are poised to follow. As of this writing, there are over 100 fee-based online music services worldwide.

The world of downloads will continue see a battle of audio file formats and digital rights management (DRM) schemes; between AAC, the format supported by Apple Computer, and WMA, the format supported by Microsoft. At present, the world of portable music players and music jukebox software is fractured by this split, resulting in compatibility problems and confusion. Despite this, sales of portable music players will continue to grow at a brisk pace.

Portability Will Increase

Right now, one of the main drawbacks of online music services is their lack of portability. This will change in the near future. Plans are in the works to provide subscription-based access to large collections of downloads that can be tethered to a portable music player. This way you'll be able to tote a jukebox of 10,000 songs around with you for a flat monthly fee of, say ten or fifteen dollars. This is attractive when you consider that filling a portable music player with that many purchased downloads at a price of $0.99 per track would cost $9,900.

Longer-term, wireless access to online music services will be enabled by technical and regulatory changes that will expand the availability of the radio spectrum for wireless uses. This means that home computers, stereos, portable music players, and even portable phones will be able to access these services using the airwaves. The celestial jukebox, as once envisioned, may be closer than we think!

Institutions Will Buy Online Music

While preparing this edition of *The Music Internet Untangled,* I noticed that many of the future possibilities discussed in the last edition are already happening. Students at the University of Pennsylvania and the University of Rochester now have high-speed access to Napster's online jukebox of 700,000 songs from their dormitories; twenty other colleges have signed similar agreements. In Denver, public library patrons are listening to Classical.com's collection of classical music from home. To login, they simply use their name and library card number. Internet service providers are buying online music too: customers of SBC'S DSL service listen to LAUNCHcast's premium internet radio service for no extra charge. In restaurants and diners across the country, patrons are using pay-for-play kiosks to access online music jukeboxes.

These institutions are providing their customers with access to music, a trend that will continue to strengthen. It seems only a matter of time before teachers and course developers incorporate on-demand music into their curricula. Students will be able to listen to assigned music anywhere they have a connection to the Internet. Likewise, hospitals and nursing homes could make the lives of their patients better by providing access to online music. I, for one, would be a happier patient knowing I could access a huge library of music while confined to my bed.

Tools for Finding Music Will Improve

At present, most online music services will let you search for music by song title, artist name, and album title. But more options are on the way. Search engines have been developed to find music using a wider range of attributes, including such things as genre, mood, tempo, and the content of lyrics. An example can be found at Soundflavor.com (now in beta release), where the advanced search form (http://soundflavor.com/Pages/FilterBuilder.aspx) lets you search for songs using over twenty attributes.

Another interesting tool has been created by a company called Predixis. A software plug-in for *Musicmatch Jukebox,* it uses algorithms to create an acoustic profile of each song in your digital music collection. You then select a song or a playlist and it will create a new mix, comprised of acoustically similar songs taken from your collection. For people with large collections of digital music, it helps to answer the question, "What shall I listen to today?"

Similar technology is helping record companies to decide which music to promote. For example, a company called PolyphonicHMI claims that its software *Hit Song Science* was able to predict the success of Norah Jones' recent hit, "Come Away With Me", by using algorithms to compare it with Top 40 hits from past years. More recently, media reports have linked this software with the production of a hit dance song in Europe. That musical tastes could be dissected in such a calculated way is an affront to many who view music appreciation as a quintessential human activity, not reducible to "mere formulas." Yet it seems inevitable that such research will help us better understand our musical impulses and, in so doing, give us another tool for increasing our enjoyment of music.

There's No Time Like the Present

Online music services have come a long way in the past two years. In both quality and number they have blossomed. They've gone from fringe to mainstream. And though further improvements lie just over the horizon, you'd be missing out if you didn't jump in now and start using some of these services. There is too much great music waiting to be discovered. If you're the type who needs a concrete plan to get going, then consult Part Three, *Internet Music Discovery Plans*. There, you'll find step-by-step plans for getting started with Internet music services and using them to discover new music.

Part Two

Music Information on the Internet

17

Using Music Information on the Internet

Traveling the road of musical discovery requires more than listening to music. We need to read. Reviews, critical essays, artist biographies, and discographies help us better understand the music and decide what to listen to. Luckily for us, Internet services have put them online and made them easily accessible. These are the tools of the music explorer, and their most important function is to help us find great music we never thought existed. They help us look beyond the small collection of industry-sanctioned stars and find the great artists that don't have fat promotion budgets. They help us sort through the thousands of new albums released every year and make choices about what to listen to. What's more, they help us become educated about what we are listening to—allowing us to better appreciate the music and everything that goes into it.

While music streams through your Internet connection, you can use your mouse and keyboard to call up rich information about the music you are listening to. You can use that same mouse and keyboard to connect with people who share your musical interests; to discuss the music you enjoy; and to find out what other people think about your favorite music. In the past, getting this kind of information required a lot of time and commitment. Today, this can be a casual activity, something that people with limited time (read: you) can easily do. In other words, you don't have to hang out at the record store with the music geeks.

While the better online music services provide good music information, they will only get you so far. The chapters that follow discuss a number of Web sites that can be used to answer your specific questions about albums, artists, songs, and music genres. These Web sites build on what the Internet music services provide. Knowing about these tools, and understanding what they can do, will help you track down new music worth caring about.

18

Finding Album Reviews

For most people, buying CDs is a hit-or-miss proposition. Out of the thousands of CDs you have the option of buying—how do you make sure you are buying the right ones? Online there is information you can use to tilt the odds in your favor. Whether it's finding albums or artists you're more likely to enjoy or finding something new to catch your interest, online information will help to increase your listening pleasure. Consider the following situations:

- You hear a good song from a band you've never heard before and you want to know more about their music.

- You're listening to a great new album. You wonder what other people think about it. You want to learn more about it.

- You're using an on-demand music service and are interested in playing music by a particular artist. Over ten different albums are available to you. Which one should you play first?

- Your online music service provides access to three albums from an artist out of twenty the artist is known to have released. Are any of them representative of that artist's best work? Would it be fair to judge the artist based on this work alone?

- You're thinking of buying an album. You wonder, "Is it worth it?"

First Stop: The Allmusic Web site - http://www.allmusic.com

The first place I go when I want answers to these questions is the Allmusic Web site, the most comprehensive and well-designed music information service on the Web—which also happens to be free.

A review of an artist's discography on the Allmusic Web site will tell you how each of their albums has been rated on a scale of one-to-five stars by Allmusic critics. In some cases, an album will be designated as an "AMG Pick," which means that it is considered "most representative" of the artist's work. Such a record will have a check mark placed next to its star rating. These ratings help you decide what to look at first, but it's the reviews that are ultimately most useful. They concisely describe the impression left by a particular record and where it stands within the artist's body of work.

Figure 18.1. Allmusic Album Review

Kind of Blue

Artist	Miles Davis
Album Title	Kind of Blue
Date of Release	Mar 2, 1959 - Apr 22, 1959 (recording)
AMG Rating	★★★★★
Genre	Jazz
Tones	Elegant, Cerebral, Intimate, Restrained, Laid-Back/Mellow, Sensual
Styles	Hard Bop, Modal Music
Time	55:16
Charts & Awards	Click here for Billboard Chart Positions & GRAMMY Awards
Product Purchase	Click here to buy this album 
	Click here to buy posters

AMG REVIEW

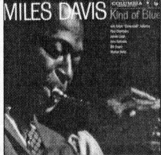

Kind of Blue isn't merely an artistic highlight for Miles Davis, it's an album that towers above its peers, a record generally considered as *the* definitive jazz album, a universally acknowledged standard of excellence. Why does *Kind of Blue* posses such a mystique? Perhaps because this music never flaunts its genius. It lures listeners in with the slow, luxurious bass line and gentle piano chords of "So What." From that moment on, the record never really changes pace — each tune has a similar relaxed feel, as the music flows easily. Yet *Kind of Blue* is more than easy listening. It's the pinnacle of modal jazz — tonality and solos build from the overall key, not chord changes, giving the music a subtly shifting quality. All of this doesn't quite explain why seasoned jazz fans return to this record even after they've memorized every nuance. They return because this is an exceptional band — Miles, Coltrane, Bill Evans, Cannonball Adderly, Paul Chambers, Jimmy Cobb — one of the greatest in history, playing at the peak of its power. As Evans said in the original liner notes for the record, the band did not play through any of these pieces prior to recording. Davis laid out the themes before the tape rolled, and then the band improvised. The end results were wondrous and still crackle with vitality. *Kind of Blue* works on many different levels. It can be played as background music, yet it amply rewards close listening. It is advanced music that is extraordinarily enjoyable. It may be a stretch to say that if you don't like *Kind of Blue*, you don't like jazz — but it's hard to imagine it as anything other than a cornerstone of *any* jazz collection. — **Stephen Thomas Erlewine**

You may find yourself using Allmusic reviews without knowing it, especially if you use online services that make use of their information. As of this writing, this includes Musicmatch, MSN Radio, and Napster. Even then, you may prefer to use the Allmusic Web site, which provides richer information and more options for browsing music. These include the ability to browse music by genre, style, mood, theme, and even instrument.

Second Stop: Amazon.com - http://www.amazon.com/music

If the Allmusic Web site doesn't review a particular album—or if I'm looking for multiple takes on an album—my next stop is the Amazon.com Web site. Although it is primarily known as an online bookseller, Amazon.com has applied to music the same combination of rich editorial information and customer reviews that helped it become the number-one destination for book shoppers. While it provides professionally written "editorial" reviews like the Allmusic site—it is the customer-written reviews that set Amazon.com apart. These reviews are more numerous and cover more recordings than those provided by any other Web site.

What's more, Amazon.com's system of allowing readers to rate the helpfulness of customer-written reviews ensures that the reviews deemed most helpful can be easily found. This is necessary as many recordings have over 100(!) reviews. The best of these reviews are easily on a par with those written by professional critics, and are often more detailed and lengthy than what you'd see in a professional review. Also, Amazon.com does a good job in allowing you to navigate through this information, providing a composite star rating of all reviews, and ways to sort reviews by star ratings, or by rated helpfulness. Collectively they provide the insights of a group of people—allowing you to get different perspectives on the same work.

Another nice feature is the ability to sort reviews by how positive or negative they are, which makes it easy for you to seek out perspectives from both the pro and con positions—something that can be educational. My understanding of favorite albums, for example, has been improved by reading intelligent criticisms that come from the negative side of the ledger. If you're really interested in an album and want to hear lots of peoples' thoughts on it—then seek out the ALL CUSTOMER REVIEWS link on Amazon.com.

Here are two reviews of the Miles Davis album, *Kind of Blue*, written by Amazon.com customers: one positive, the other negative.

Amazon.com Customer Review of *Kind of Blue*: Pro

⭐⭐⭐⭐⭐ **The Cornerstone of Any Jazz Collection**, February 19, 2000
Reviewer: misterd40 (see more about me) from Rancho Cucamonga, CA USA
This is the cornerstone of any jazz collection; this is the place to begin if you are a jazz neophyte. If you are unfamiliar with jazz this is probably what you imagine jazz sounds like. Miles Davis was important not only for the great music he made but also for the incomparable sideman he worked with-such as saxophonist John Coltrane, here. From the classic, swinging opening bars of "So What" to Miles' signature muted trumpet in the ballad, "Blue and Green" this CD best summarizes all that is great about jazz. Over the last few years the Columbia/Legacy label has begun an incomparable reissue program of Miles Davis' 50s and 60s albums. This, and the other reissues, contain restored cover artwork, great re-mastered sound, original liner notes and current reflections on Miles' work. The sound re-mastering on this CD is first class. You will hardly believe that this was recorded in 1959-the sound is so clear and warm. I cannot recommend this CD enough!

Amazon.com Customer Review of *Kind of Blue*: Con

⭐ **No, no, no!**, April 17, 2001
Reviewer: **A music fan** from New York, NY USA
If pretension, tedium, and self-indulgence are your idea of what should animate music, then this is the album and Miles Davis is the "artist" for you. If you think music should be invigorating and joyful and make its listeners feel great, then try something else--early "hot" jazz like Jelly Roll Morton, Louis Armstrong and the Hot Five and/or Hot Seven, Bix Beiderbecke, Fats Waller, or even later swing and big band music. Jazz was once extremely popular--back when the music was fun. Today, jazz is the worst selling genre in all of popular music. No one cares about modern jazz except would-be elitists who don't even like music so much as they like the cachet they mistakenly think they get when they affect to like someone like Miles Davis--a man who probably did more than anyone else to kill off jazz and wrap it in its current cocoon of irrelevance.

Next Stop: Google - http://www.google.com

Whether they be professional or amateur, there is no shortage of published opinions about music. There are scores of review sources that can be consulted once the Allmusic and Amazon.com Web sites have been exhausted. The quickest way to tap into them is to enter a search into the Google search engine, consisting of the following elements:

- The word *review*
- The name of the record searched as a phrase (with quote marks around it)
- The name of the artist searched as a phrase (with quote marks around it)

For example, to search for a review of the surfer band Pollo Del Mar's album, *The Ocean is Not for Cowards,* I would go to the Google site and submit the following query into the search box:

review "pollo del mar" "the ocean is not for cowards"

Although neither the Allmusic nor Amazon.com Web sites had reviews for this album, I was able to find a least two reviews by scanning the results of this Google search. This doesn't always work—but has succeeded often enough for me. Of course this approach can be used with other Internet search engines besides Google.

Other Record Review Archives

Some reviews are can be found in the "Invisible Web", in databases whose contents are not visible to general purpose search engines like Google. To find these reviews, you need to go to the Web site in question and use their search engine. The following sites contain review archives you can consult:

Classical Reviews

- **Gramofile** - http://www.gramofile.co.uk/cdreviews.asp
  30,000+ reviews of classical recordings produced by the makers of *Gramophone*, the classical music magazine. Registration is required.

Rock & Pop Reviews

- **MetaCritic Music Reviews** - http://www.metacritic.com/music
  This site aggregates reviews from other sources so that you can review a range of critical opinions about a given album. Highly recommended.

- **The Onion AV Club** - http://www.theonionavclub.com/archives/music
  A sizeable collection of reviews, brought to you by the publishers of the humor Web site, The Onion.

- **Pitchfork** - http://pitchforkmedia.com/record-reviews
  Searchable and browseable archive from the U.S. based Pitchfork Media site, "home of the gratuitously in-depth record review."

- **Pop Matters** - http://www.popmatters.com/music/reviews/archive-a.html
  Reviews from a Chicago based "magazine of global culture."

- **Q Magazine Reviews** - http://www.q4music.com/nav?page=q4music.review
  For a U.K. perspective, 20,000+ reviews from *Q Magazine*.

- **Rolling Stone** - http://rollingstone.com/reviews/cd/cds_az.asp
  Reviews from the magazine—includes reader responses and ratings. Reviews can be browsed by release date, star rating, or artist name.

- **Robert Cristgau Consumer Guide** - http://robertchristgau.com/cg.php
  10,000+ capsule reviews from *Village Voice* critic Robert Cristgau, "Dean of American Rock Critics."

- **Trouser Press Reviews** - http://www.trouserpress.com
  Reviews taken from the well regarded Trowser Press Guides, covering the '70s, '80s, and '90s. Highly recommended.

- **75 or Less** - http://www.75orless.com
  Where brevity is a virtue. Every review is 75 words or fewer.

The Internet and the Rise of the Amateur Critic

As with other topics, the Internet has made it easy for enthusiasts to publish their opinions about music online. Though the quality of this outpouring varies, the amount of new material is impressive and worth tapping into. Further, sites like Amazon.com and Epinions.com have developed systems to highlight the best reviews and reviewers. With no shortage of professional critics writing reviews, why take the time to read these reviews? First, no one else may have reviewed the recording. Second, you can get multiple perspectives on one recording: some positive, some negative. Even if you like an album, it can be useful to read negative reviews to get other perspectives. Last, the best of these reviews easily stack up to professionally written reviews. Passionate fans can bring to bear an encyclopedic knowledge of the artist, an attention to the tiniest of details, and a true love for the artist's music that a professional reviewer would be hard pressed to match.

Jazz Reviews

- **JazzReview.com** - http://www.jazzreview.com/reviewsearchpage.cfm
  Over 4,900 reviews of jazz albums from a Web portal devoted to jazz information.

Take Reviews with a Grain of Salt

Buying simply on the strength of rave reviews can lead to disappointment. Similarly, it is possible to love albums that are scorned by the critics. Reviews are, after all, the product of individuals whose tastes may be different from yours. The listening experience is subjective; the same album played at a different time, at a different place can seem totally different—even to the same person. As a result, it is insufficient to rely on simplistic "star " ratings (e.g., three out of five stars). While easy to digest, these ratings only tell you how much a reviewer liked a recording, not why he or she liked it or what the music is like. Good reviews tell you this and more. A good review will go beyond the reviewer's personal response to the music and help you understand the work, the circumstances behind its making, and its place within the artist's body of work. It will also draw comparisons with other musical works—and assess the work's significance to the broader culture. Use them as tools not crutches. They will save you time, but won't relieve you of the task of listening to and judging the music for yourself—which is, after all, where much of the fun lies!

19

Using Best-of Lists

In the movie *High Fidelity*, a record shop owner named Rob (played by John Cusack) expresses his worldview in the form of "Top 5" lists: his five best "side-one track-one" songs of all-time, his five best movies of all time, his five favorite books, etc. When talking about other people, such as former girlfriends on his top five "most memorable split-ups" list, he sizes them up in terms of their "top fives." Later, he tells the audience, "It's *what* you like that counts, not what you *are* like."

Best-of lists condense a number of critical opinions into a brief, easy-to-read format. For many of us, these lists make compelling reading—as they allow us to satisfy our curiosity about the music other people think is best and whether our own favorites make the grade. If we don't like what we see, we can always make our own list! Also, lists that attempt to summarize the best music of an era are a great way to learn which albums are considered part of the "canon" of popular music—albums we need to know about if we are to consider ourselves knowledgeable about popular music. Remember, though—a list without some explanation as to why items were included is of limited use, simplistic in the same way that "star" album ratings are when not accompanied by reviews that explain the rating.

Types of Lists

- **Annual Best-of Lists**
  At the end of each year, music critics publish their "top picks" in newspapers, magazines, and most every publication or Web site that regularly publishes music reviews. They list the selected albums and usually include brief explanations on why each selection was chosen. Watch for these in your review publication of choice. Some Web sites, such as the Acclaimed Music Web site (http://www.acclaimedmusic.net), accumulate links to current best-of lists on the Web.

- **All-Time Greatest Lists**
  These lists attempt to make definitive statements about the best music of all-time or, in some cases, the best music from a given era. These are good for stirring up debate. Most often they are published by music magazines, and involve either the editorial judgment of the magazine staff or polls of critics or fans. In addition, some Web sites (such as the Acclaimed Music Web site mentioned above) have created composite "all-time" ratings by combining and weighting the results from multiple lists.

- **Best-of Lists by Genre or Artists**
  Amazon.com's "Essential CDs" lists provide this type of information. To find them, select the "Essential CDs" option on Amazon.com's music home page. Some magazines also publish genre specific lists.

- **Beginner's Lists**
  Often seen on Classical Music sites. One example is Classical.net's Basic Repertoire List at: http://www.classical.net/music/rep/top.html.

- **Thematic Lists**
  These lists are more particular in focus—and may not even be best-of lists. A fun Web site for reading such lists is the Rock Critic's Top Five Lists site: http://www.rockcritics.com/topfive. Here you find lists such as, *Five songs that should be made into feature length movies,* to which you are invited to add your selections and comments. You can also create you own list topic, to which others can add their versions and comments. As this book went to press, this site was in the process of finding a new home (different servers) and the Top Five Lists site was offline. With any luck, they will be back online by the time you read this.

- **Fan-Created Lists**
  This is where the fans get their say. A good source of such lists is the Amazon.com Web site, which gives its customers the freedom to engage in "Listmania." Here, users can create annotated lists of any products being sold on the Web site—including CDs and books. These lists can be based on any theme or selection criteria the list creator wishes. Like fan-written reviews, they vary in quality. The better ones can be useful to the music explorer. To access them, you need to be browsing CDs on the Amazon.com Web site. If there are Listmania lists that include the CD you are looking at, you'll see links to these lists near the bottom of the page.

Best-of Radio Programs

If the true test of a best-of list is to be found in the listening, then the ideal best-of list is one that you can listen to. Taking a cue from old-time Top-40 countdown shows, some Internet music services have taken best-of lists and translated them into radio broadcasts—which allow listeners to sample "the best" according to the list in question. Examples include:

- **Rhapsody's "Best of 2003" station**
  Rhapsody staff's selections for the best albums of 2003 in various genres. A "Best of 2002" station is also available. For Rhapsody subscribers.

- **Rolling Stone's Immortals Station (on Rhapsody)**
  "The music of the 50 greatest artists of all time, as selected by a panel of musicians, producers and critics." For Rhapsody subscribers.

- **Radio VH1's 100 Greatest Series**
  These collections have been assembled by VH1 staff and "music critics and journalists." Registration is required to access these stations.

  -100 Greatest Songs of Rock and Roll
    http://www.vh1.com/music/radio/stations/100_greatest_rock_songs/station.jhtml

  -100 Greatest Women of Rock and Roll
    http://www.vh1.com/music/radio/stations/100_greatest_rock_women/station.jhtml

  -100 Greatest Hard Rock Artists
    http://www.vh1.com/music/radio/stations/100_greatest_rock_artists/station.jhtml

  -100 Greatest Dance Songs
    http://www.vh1.com/music/radio/stations/100_greatest_dance_songs/station.jhtml

  -100 Greatest Albums of Rock and Roll
    http://www.vh1.com/music/radio/stations/100_greatest_rock_albums/station.jhtml

  -100 Greatest Love Songs
    http://www.vh1.com/music/radio/stations/100_greatest_love_songs/station.jhtml

Best-of Radio Stations List

With so many Internet radio stations to choose from, "best-of" lists can help steer us to promising stations.

- **Best of Live365** - http://www.live365.com/community/awards_winners.html
  Listeners vote for the best Live365 stations in categories by genre and size of station. These "Mikey" awards give listeners another way to pick stations to try from among the thousands that are available on Live365. Awards have been handed out in 45 categories.

Notable Web Sites with Best-of Information

- **Metacritic** - http://metacritic.com/music
  Reviews "from up to 30 national publications" are weighted and combined to produce a "Metascore" for albums. Ranked lists are provided for the years 2000 through 2003 as well as for "all albums reviewed." A list of review publications used is provided. Metacritic provides similar ranked listings for movies and video games.

- **Acclaimed Music Site** - http://www.acclaimedmusic.net
  The product of one Swede's obsession with best-of lists, this site provides easy access to a huge array of best-of popular music lists from around the world. It is a great source for international best-of lists. Composite "all-time" rankings are also provided, as are listings indexed by album name, artist name, and year. Be prepared to wade through pop-up ads though, as this site is run on a "free" Web hosting service.

- **Pitchfork's Best New Music** - http://www.pitchforkmedia.com/best
  This Web page lists, in reverse chronological order, the best new albums as reviewed on the Pitchfork Web site. Each album listing has a numerical rating, a genre label, a capsule review, and a link to the longer, "full review."

20

Using Music Awards To Find Out What's Hot

Not willing to sit through an evening-long show to find out who won the Grammy awards? Well, neither am I. Although music award shows focus primarily on the performers, "best album" awards are also given and are of interest to music fans. Some awards, such as the American Music Awards, are based on popular vote by fans. Other awards are based on selections made by music professionals or critics. A few of note include:

- **Grammy Awards** - http://grammy.aol.com/awards
  Yearly awards for artistic and technical achievement awarded by the Los Angeles-based Recording Academy. Over 100 awards are given in twenty-eight categories of music (Pop, Gospel, Classical, etc.) including "best album" in each category. Voting members are professionals with creative or technical credits on six commercially released tracks (or their equivalent). Awards can be searched back to 1958, the year the awards started. *Note*: VH1 radio has a Grammy Awards-focused radio station that allows you to hear music by current Grammy award nominated artists. Virgin Free Radio has a similar station.

- **Mercury Music Prize** - http://www.mercurymusicprize.com
  An independent panel of judges selects British "Albums of the Year" across a range of genres, which leads to the eventual selection of one album and performer as the Mercury Music Prize recipient. The site and the award process are a marvel of simplicity when compared to the Grammys.

- **Gramophone Awards** - http://www.gramophone.co.uk/currentwin.asp
  Presented in the fall in London each year, these are considered the "Oscars of the classical music world." Voting is done by a committee of Gramophone reviewers and specialist critics. Approximately twenty awards are given, including Artist of the Year and Recording of the Year. Award information going back to 1977 is available.

Of course there are scores of other awards that focus on particular genres of music or which are handed out in a particular country. Many of these can be found on the corresponding directory pages on Google or Yahoo:

- **Yahoo Award listings** - http://dir.yahoo.com/Entertainment/Music/Awards

- **Google Award listings** - http://directory.google.com/Top/Arts/Music/Awards

---

Two Measures of Importance: Popularity and Critical Acclaim

Just because the critics love something doesn't mean the music-buying public will buy it. At the same time many recordings that are popular get little, if any, critical respect. This highlights the difference between critical acclaim and popularity, both of which are valid measures of an album's importance. Critical acclaim is found in the writings of critics, whereas popularity is measured on record sales and radio airplay charts.

Critical acclaim reflects the assessments of educated and knowledgeable music aficionados. A good critic will help you understand a piece of music, as well as the artist performing it, and will illuminate the strengths and weaknesses of a given piece as compared to similar music. At the same time, many people are less interested in what the critics think—and are more interested in what their fellow listeners and record buyers think. Hence they focus on the charts. Charts and record reviews are both useful to the music explorer—but it is best to understand the limitations of each and use them accordingly.

21

Using Music Charts
To Find Out What's Hot

Want to know what's popular? The music charts will tell you. This includes album sales charts, which measure retail album sales, and radio airplay charts, which measure how often songs are included in radio playlists. These charts are created by the music industry, which uses them to measure the commercial success of music being promoted and sold within the industry system. Beyond their use as an industry scoreboard, music charts can be used to:

* Identify new artists and music to try out

* Learn what other people are listening to

* Stay on top of trends in popular music

* Stay current with the music celebrities du jour and who's "on top"

There are charts for singles and charts for albums. There are charts for major genres of music, and charts for specific countries. The most recognized sales charts in the United States are the Billboard charts. Another kind of chart, the Gracenote Digital charts, measures the number of times that Internet-connected people play a given song using their music player software. This is arguably a better way to measure popularity because it measures the tracks people choose to play, whereas sales charts simply measure purchase transactions. Think of all the albums that collect dust after a single playing. Likewise, radio airplay charts measure popularity based on how often radio programmers choose to play music, not the actual preferences of the listeners.

Chart Sites of Note

* **Billboard Charts** - http://www.billboard.com/billboard/charts/index.jsp
  These charts track sales of U.S. albums and singles by genre. Also provided are charts of top grossing concerts and top videos. A "heatseekers" chart lists best selling titles by artists who have yet to have a Top 100 album. A fee-based version, aimed at music industry people, provides more detailed charts. A weekly top 100 countdown show, *Billboard Radio,* is webcast from this site. Historical Billboard charts are available on both the Napster and iTunes Music Store services.

- **Gracenote Digital Top 10** - http://www.gracenote.com/music/topten.html
  The Gracenote Digital Top 10 lists the most frequent played albums on the Internet, aggregated weekly from over 30 million listeners worldwide using the Gracenote CDDB® Music Recognition Service. Additional charts cover the following categories: Rock, Urban, World, Country/Folk, Electronic/Dance, Jazz, Soundtrack and CCM/Gospel music. The Gracenote Top Digital 20 is available as a weekly free e-mail newsletter.

- **U.K. Charts** - http://www.bbc.co.uk/radio1/chart/top40/index.shtml
  Charts in the following categories are provided: Singles, Albums, Compilations, Rock, R&B, and Indie. The most recent U.K. top 40 countdown show is recorded and available for listening.

- **Mobile Beat Top 200** - http://www.mobilebeat.com/top200.asp
  Consult this list to see what working disc jockeys in the U.S. are getting the most requests for. Based on a yearly poll conducted by *Mobile Beat* magazine, this list shows what music is getting played at weddings, parties, and other events being serviced by the "mobile DJ."

Other Sources of Chart Information

The following directory pages provide links to charts from all over the world:

- **Google Listings** - http://directory.google.com/Top/Arts/Music/Charts

- **Yahoo Listings** - http://dir.yahoo.com/Entertainment/Music/Charts

---

About Chart Watching

Although there are plenty of music aficionados who aren't particularly interested in what the masses are buying, there is in chart watching something that appeals to deep-seated human impulses. Popular music charts and the commentary and radio countdown programs that accompany them have an element of drama and soap opera to them. Who's on the rise? Who's falling? Who are the Cinderellas and one-hit wonders? Charts record in black and white the trajectories of artists' careers—their milestones, their high-water marks, and their commercial legacy. As such, chart performances become part of pop music history and are followed in much the way that box scores, win-loss records, and batting averages are followed by baseball fans—at least to those who are drawn to the numbers.

22

Song Information
What Are They Saying?

Song lyrics are more important to some people than others. Most often, I focus on how the sound makes me feel rather than on what the songwriter is trying to tell me. There are times, however, when I love a song enough to really want to know what the words say. That's when it's handy to track down lyrics. Lyrics are sometimes printed on the liner notes that come with a CD, but very often are not. Online music services haven't done much with lyrics either. This leaves us to hunt around on the Web, which is a distinctly hit or miss proposition. The more popular the artist, the greater the chances you'll find their lyrics online—either on an artist's Web site, a fan Web site, or on a general purpose lyrics Web site.

While numerous lyrics search engines exist, none of them provide access to as many lyrics as do the major, Internet-wide search engines, such as Google. So that's where I start, by doing a search using the following elements:

- The word *lyrics*
- The name of the song searched as a phrase (with quote marks around it)
- The name of the artist searched as a phrase (with quote marks around it)

For example, to search for the lyrics of the song "A Sailor's Life", performed by the band Fairport Convention, I would go to Google (http://www.google.com) and enter the following query into the search box:

lyrics "a sailor's life" "fairport convention"

Then browse the search results and most of the time—assuming the artist is popular—you will find the lyrics. If you don't know the name of the song, but you know a unique bit of the lyrics (a phrase or a chorus) you could insert that in place of the song's name—also with quote marks around it. Alternately, if you are looking to find discussions about a song by fans or critics you might conduct exactly the same search but omit the word "lyrics."

If this fails, another option is to try the available Lyrics search engines. A list of these can be found on Yahoo: http://dir.yahoo.com/Entertainment/Music/Lyrics.

A word of caution: many of these lyrics sites will bombard you with pop-up ads and offers to install "useful" pieces of software that are little more than spyware. If you are prepared to swat these annoyances away, you will often find the lyrics you are looking for.

Another option is to try to locate a fan site for the artist. Even if it doesn't contain the lyrics you are looking for, it will probably provide the means for contacting other fans to see if they can supply the lyrics. Two services providing interesting information about songs are LAUNCHcast and MSN Music:

- **LAUNCHcast's "Search for Lyrics" Link**
  LAUNCHcast is the only major service that attempts to help you find lyrics. Clicking on their SEARCH FOR LYRICS link (available on the player) launches a Yahoo search for the lyrics of the song you are listening to. This doesn't guarantee you'll find the lyrics, but does save you the effort of running a separate search. Also, by clicking on the song name, you will be taken to a song information page, where you can see a list of other LAUNCHcast users who are fans of that song, as well as links to their personal radio stations.

- **MSN Radio Plus' SoundsLike Feature**
  MSN Radio Plus also lets you click on a song name to get more information. In this case you get information on the album in question, as well as the option to VIEW SOUNDSLIKE SONGS. By clicking on this option, MSN will return a list of songs that "sound like" the one in question.

Songs Lost in the Translation: KissThisGuy.com

If you've ever butchered the lyrics to a popular song, or embarrassed yourself in public by singing the wrong lyrics out loud, take heart: you've got company. There's a Web site to prove it: http://kissthisguy.com. This site gets its name from a misheard Jimi Hendrix lyric, "excuse me while I kiss the sky" and tells a story of how Jimi used the "wrong" version for fun in some of his concerts. View misheard lyrics from over 1000 songs by artist and by song title. You have the option of adding your own, along with your story of how it happened and whether you were able to convince other people that your version was right.

23

Behind the Music
Questions about Artists

When you hear a great song by somebody you've never heard before, it's a natural impulse to ask, "Who was that?" and "What else have they done?" Sometimes we just want to know more about them. To answer these questions, we need access to artist biographies and discographies.

The AllMusic Web Site: Good for Artist Information Too

Although Allmusic biographies are available from a number of online music services—including Musicmatch, Napster, and MSN Radio—I prefer using the Allmusic Web site (http://www.allmusic.com) because the information there is richer. For each artist, you learn when he or she was active and get information about where they fit in the wider world of music. This includes:

• GENRES	Major genre or genres of music performed
• STYLES	Sub-genres or styles of music performed
• INSTRUMENTS	Instruments played (for individual artists only)
• MOODS	Adjectives used to describe this music
• CHARTS/AWARDS	Billboard chart position(s) and Grammy awards
• SIMILAR ARTISTS	Artists who play similar music
• INFLUENCED BY	Artists who influenced this artist
• FOLLOWERS	Artists influenced by this artist
• PERFORMED SONGS BY	Songwriters whose work they have performed

What is especially remarkable is that each related-artist entry is hyperlinked to an Allmusic Web page devoted to that artist. This means you can easily read up on related artists and explore the broader world of music that a particular artist is connected to.

Also available is a discography section, which lists, by release date, the albums an artist has released. Each listing provides a star rating, a link to a review (if available), and a BUY link which let you purchase the CD from Barnes and Noble. The discography also lists compilations, singles, EPs, DVDs, and videos (if available). Bootleg recordings are sometimes also listed.

Figure 23.1. Allmusic artist page for Sandy Denny - Overview Tab

Figure 23.2. Allmusic artist page for Sandy Denny - Discography Tab

Rating	Year ▲	Title	Label
★★★☆☆	1968	All Our Own Work	Pickwick
★★★☆☆	1970	Sandy Denny [Saga]	Saga
★★★☆☆	1971	North Star Grassman and the Ravens	Hannibal
★★★★☆	1972	Sandy	A&M
★★☆☆☆	1972	The Bunch	A&M
★★☆☆☆	1973	Like an Old Fashioned Waltz	Hannibal
★★★☆☆	1977	Rendezvous	Hannibal
★★★☆☆	1978	Original Sandy Denny	Trojan
★★★★☆	1985	Sandy Denny & The Strawbs	Hannibal
★★★☆☆	2000	Listen Listen	Polygram International
		Sandy Denny, Trevor Lucas	Special Delivery

Finding an Artist's Most Important Work

A review of the discography and an examination of both the star ratings and the reviews will give you a sense of which albums the Allmusic critics think are most important to listen to. As mentioned elsewhere, this kind of assessment is subjective, but often there is agreement among music critics as to which albums constitute an artist's most important contributions to the canon of popular music. Of course from an industry perspective the most important albums are the bestselling ones, but that isn't necessarily the same thing.

One helpful attempt at compiling a list of "essential" recordings by artist can be found at Amazon.com's "Essential CDs" page, which can be found on the Amazon.com music menu (see Figure 23.3). Essential CD lists are compiled in the following categories: by artist, by music style, by year, and for classical music, by composer. While they don't tell you what the criteria for being "essential" are—and I did note at least one troubling omission for one of my favorite artists—I do think the lists are useful, particularly for artists with lots of albums to choose from. The artists covered tend to be major artists. For more obscure artists you can use the Amazon.com customer ratings and reviews, as well as other review sources, to aid in your decision-making.

Figure 23.3. Essential CDs link on Amazon.com music menu

Classical Artist Information

The BBC's Classical Web site (http://www.bbc.co.uk/music/muze/classical.shtml) provides access to biographical entries from the *Grove Concise Dictionary of Music*, a highly respected reference source. Also available are detailed profiles of major classical artists (other genres are covered as well). Each profile provides pithy summaries of the artist (e.g., "Mahler in One Minute"), links to biography and discography information, and brief lists of "good recordings" and "good reads" (recommended books). Also useful is an archive of the *Discovering Music on Radio 3* show, in which presenters "explore the depths of a major classical work, to explain what makes it a masterpiece." Over 100 shows are available on-demand in RealAudio format. The listing is sorted by composer. The URL is: http://www.bbc.co.uk/radio3/discoveringmusic/audioarchive.shtml.

The Allmusic Web site also covers composers and performers of Classical music. Its All Classical Web site was recently folded into the main Allmusic site.

Digging Deeper: You've Become a Fan

When your appreciation for an artist—or perhaps simple fascination—reaches a certain level, you become a fan, willing to devote real time to understanding their music and learning more about them. Now is the time to venture into artist Web sites. Artist Web sites come in different flavors:

- **"Official" record company Web sites**
  Primarily concerned with marketing the artist, these sites tend to be slick, but are not necessarily the most informative. Some are quite good.

- **Fan-created Web sites**
  These are labors of love, created by fans wanting to publicly celebrate the genius of their favorite artists. While often less attractive than the professionally produced record company sites, these sites are often the richest sources of online information about an artist. It helps to be obsessed! These sites vary in quality and there might be numerous fan sites for a popular artist. So it pays to scope them out and see which one(s) are best.

- **Artist-created Web sites**
Lesser-known artists often produce their own sites. Designed for marketing purposes, these sites will often have touring schedules, band updates, and links to buy CDs and merchandise. Some artists use these sites to communicate with their fans—posting letters and tour diaries, or in some cases hosting chats. In other cases individual band members might have separate Web sites, with information about side projects, personal interests, etc.

Information you can find on artist Web sites includes:

• REVIEWS	• FAN ART	• MESSAGE BOARDS
• ARTICLES	• PHOTOS	• DISCOGRAPHIES
• INTERVIEWS	• VIDEOS	• MERCHANDISE
• GOSSIP	• STORIES	• CDS FOR SALE
• TRIVIA	• BAND LORE	• CONTESTS
• RUMORS	• TOUR DATES	• FAN RECORDINGS
• SPECULATION	• MAILING LISTS	

There are two approaches I recommend to find artist Web sites:

If the artist is reasonably well known, go to Yahoo's directory of music artist Web sites (http://dir.yahoo.com/Entertainment/Music/Artists) and look up the artist. This site performs the useful service of pulling together links to multiple Web sites for a given artist. Google has a similar directory site that is also worth trying: http://directory.google.com/Top/Arts/Music/Bands_and_Artists.

If the artist or band is obscure and therefore not likely to have gained an entry in Yahoo's directory, then go to Google (http//www.google.com) and enter the name of the artist in quotations and hit enter (e.g., *Pollo Del Mar*" to find the Web site for band Pollo Del Mar). You may have to browse through a few entries to find one, if in fact one exists.

Bits and Pieces

To find a particular type of artist information—say, an interview, photos, or a video—do a Google search using the artist's name in quotes plus a word describing the kind of information you're looking for. Use the Google **OR** command to capture variants. Some examples:

To find photos of Fleetwood Mac:

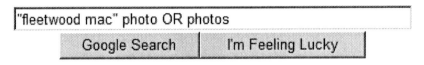

To find interviews with Mark Eitzel:

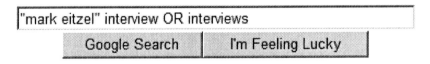

There are also Web sites with archives of photos and videos worth visiting:

- *Rolling Stone* photo archive: http://www.rollingstone.com/photos/photos_az.asp
- *Rolling Stone* Video archive: http://www.rollingstone.com/videos/videos_az.asp
- Launch Videos: http://launch.yahoo.com/musicvideos

Who Else Plays Music Like This?

Once you've exhausted what a particular artist has to offer, the logical question presents itself: "Who else plays music like this?"

One option is to consult the artist page on the Allmusic Web site for "Similar Artists" listings. Here, you find not only artists who play similar music. You will also find "Followers" who were influenced by this artist, as well as artists this artist has been "Influenced By." Each artist reference links to an artist page for that artist—great for learning more. Such listings are not available for the more obscure artists.

Another option is to look at the "Styles" listings on an Allmusic artist page. Here you will see the sub-genres of music associated with that artist. Clicking on any of these style listings will take you a Web page listing "Top Artists"—those deemed best or most representative of that particular style.

A third option is to use the artist recommendations provided by online stores and Internet music services. A technique called collaborative filtering is used to capture the preferences of a group of people and use them to predict what a given person might like based on what is known about them. The recommendations usually take the form:

People who liked this [record or artist] also tended to like the following [records or artists]

They can be useful for suggesting music to try, but take them with a grain of salt. They won't always be good recommendations. Occasionally they can be downright bizarre. Some people are offended by the notion that a computer purports to understand their "unique, individual" tastes, and so discount the usefulness of these recommendations. Others are worried about the loss of privacy and don't like the idea of their listening habits being tracked. To this group I suggest they read the privacy policies of services before agreeing to use them and where possible, opt out of personalization schemes that are too intrusive for their tastes. For example, Musicmatch lets users to opt out of their personalization scheme, which draws on play logs from the *Musicmatch Jukebox* software. On balance I think personalized recommendations, while imperfect, are helpful to the music explorer.

Another place to find related artists is Musicplasma (http://musicplasma.com), a Web site which lets you view maps showing relationships between artists. The closer the relationship, the closer the proximity on the map. More popular artists are shown to have bigger spheres or "halos" (see Figure 23.4). Using your mouse, it is possible to navigate through the maps and fly through "artist space" to find new and interesting connections. Sound clips and artist discographies are supplied, as are links to Amazon.com album pages. By clicking on the speaker icon, you can activate a stream of sound clips for the currently highlighted artist. If you click on a different artist icon, the stream of sound clips will change, playing music from the new artist. In this way, you can fly through "artist space" with your ears as well as your eyes. Other buttons let you fiddle with the look and feel of the music maps; links, color, and halos are all modifiable. This site is fun to use and well worth a visit.

Figure 23.4. Musicplasma showing artists related to Nick Cave

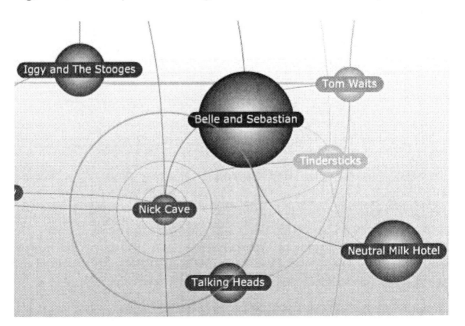

24

Learning More About Music Genres

Music today is more varied than ever before. New styles are evolving at a rapid pace, adding to an already rich catalog of existing music. This variety is both wonderful and daunting to behold; wonderful, because it means the banquet of choices keeps getting richer; daunting, because there is so much more to choose from.

An understanding of musical styles makes it easier to navigate these choices. It helps us break the world of music into understandable pieces. As much as musicians rail against being categorized—sometimes rightly so—having labels and categories gives us a common language that makes it easier to talk about music. What's more, style labels help to group related artists together and so are helpful for music discovery.

The Allmusic Site Comes to the Rescue – Again!

The Allmusic Web site's genre and style information pages mesh nicely with its artist and album information pages. Both the artist and album information pages have links to genre pages, which can also be accessed from the EXPLORE BY GENRE heading on the Allmusic home page. Access to some of this content—while still free—now requires registration.

The Allmusic genre and style pages each contain a capsule summary of the genre discussing its musical characteristics and evolution. Following this summary are lists of "top" artists, albums, and songs, selected by Allmusic's editors as the best and most representative examples of the style. See Figure 24.1 for an example. Clicking on the artist, album, or song pages will take you to an Allmusic Web page with more information. Links to fifteen second sound clips (Windows Media Player required) are also provided. In some cases, links are provided to essays written by Allmusic staff about a given genre or style.

If you're looking for essays, I recommend going to the broadest genre category pages: those for rock, jazz, country, and world music. Each of these pages provides links to at least twenty different essays on specific styles of music within the broader category. These pages contain links to style-specific essays that may not appear on the appropriate Allmusic style page. In addition to providing useful information about musical styles, these essays often recommend useful or important recordings to listen to.

Figure 24.1. Allmusic Swamp Blues Information Page

explore by.../ Blues/ Electric Blues/ ✉ Send to
explore by... **Swamp Blues**
Genre

Swamp Blues, the looser, more rhythmic variation of the standard Louisiana sound, also brings more contemporary elements of New Orleans, zydeco, soul music, and Cajun to bear on its style. The guitar wor simple but effective, and is heavily influenced by the boogie patterns used on Jimmy Reed records, with lit doses of Lightnin' Hopkins and Muddy Waters. Unlike the heavy backbeat of the more popular urban styles, rhythm can be best described as laid-back, making even its most uptempo offerings share the same mood a ambience of the most desultory of slow blues. — **Cub Koda**

Related Styles

- R&B
- New Orleans Blues
- Harmonica Blues
- Swamp Pop
- Louisiana Blues

- Juke Joint Blues
- Slide Guitar Blues
- Acoustic Texas Blues
- Acoustic Louisiana Blues
- Zydeco

- New Orleans Blues
- Swamp Pop
- Modern Electric Blues

Swamp Blues Album Highlights

🛒 buy ◀ listen   🛒 buy   🛒 buy ◀ listen   🛒 buy ◀ listen   🛒 buy ◀ listen   🛒 buy ◀ listen

Top Artists	Top Albums	Top Songs
Click here for full list.	Click here for full list.	Click here for full list.

Top Artists
- Guitar Junior ◀
- Slim Harpo ◀
- Lazy Lester ◀
- Lightnin' Slim ◀
- Nathan Abshire ◀
- Tab Benoit ◀
- Cookie & the Cupcakes ◀
- Joe Hudson ◀
- Lonesome Sundown ◀
- Whispering Smith ◀
- Katie Webster ◀
- Marcia Ball ◀
- Guitar Gable
- Larry Garner ◀
- Silas Hogan ◀
- Jerry "Boogie" McCain ◀
- Kenny Neal ◀
- Rockin' Sidney ◀

Top Albums
- I Hear You Knockin'! The Excello Singles ◀
  Lazy Lester
- Rooster Blues ◀
  Lightnin' Slim
- The Best of Slim Harpo [Hip-O] ◀
  Slim Harpo
- Crawl: Charly Blues Masterworks, Vol. 1 ◀
  Guitar Junior
- Deluxe Edition ◀
  Kenny Neal
- Deluxe Edition ◀
  Katie Webster
- Gatorhythms ◀
  Marcia Ball
- I'm a Mojo Man: The Best of the Excello Singles
  Lonesome Sundown
- King of the Swamp Blues 1954-61
  Lightnin' Slim

Top Songs
- Baby Scratch My Back ◀
  Slim Harpo
- Don't Take It So Hard ◀
  Snooks Eaglin
- Down in the Swamp ◀
  Tab Benoit
- I Got Love If You Want It ◀
  Slim Harpo
- I Hear You Knockin'
  Lazy Lester
- I'm a King Bee ◀
  Slim Harpo
- I'm a Lover Not a Fighter ◀
  Lazy Lester
- My Home Is a Prison ◀
  Lonesome Sundown
- Rooster Blues ◀
  Lightnin' Slim
- Traveling Mood ◀
  Snooks Eaglin

Music Services Good for Genre Explorations

Online jukeboxes and Internet radio services provide the best means for exploring new music genres through listening. Notable examples include:

- **Musicmatch Online**
  Musicmatch Radio users can listen to over 200 genre-based radio stations while accessing style information provided from the Allmusic Guide. Musicmatch On-Demand users can also access playlists and artist lists for the same genres. Here, the focus is on artists and albums that are most popular with other Musicmatch users.

- **Rhapsody**
  For each genre and subgenre covered, Rhapsody provides a summary of the style, a sampler playlist, and lists of key artists and albums (as determined by critical opinion), with links to the album and artist pages if available. Also listed are Rhapsody radio stations that play music from that style.

- **Live365**
  Although not as well organized as either Musicmatch Online or Rhapsody, Live365 is home to a large number of single-genre, single-theme radio stations that make it easy to conduct listening explorations of a given style. Where else are you going to find a station devoted to sea shanties?

25

Finding People
Who Share Your Interests

Certain situations call for a good conversation. You're looking for an answer to a question that can't easily be found. Or perhaps you're tired of just reading about music and you want to talk to someone about it. You want to share your enthusiasm, your knowledge, and your insights—maybe even be recognized for it. Or perhaps you just want to learn from other enthusiasts—people who have been obsessing over your favorite music for longer than you have. Whatever the motive, seeking out other people online can add a new dimension to your music enjoyment.

Communities of Interest

Online groups, or "communities of interest" as they are sometimes called, use a range of tools to facilitate their exchanges. The most useful are e-mail-based discussion groups and Web-based message boards, which allow you to follow discussions over time and post messages whenever it's convenient. The better online groups have guidelines that dictate what topics are fair game for discussion and what topics aren't. For example, a group devoted to discussion of Baroque music probably doesn't want to hear about the latest Britney Spears release—or see somebody's new recipe for chocolate chip cookies (however tasty). This helps to keep things focused. Also helpful are message archives, which allow you to see if your question has already been answered. Some groups will put together a list of frequently asked questions, or FAQs, with answers for the benefit of new members.

Yahoo Groups

The largest repository of music discussion groups can be found in the Yahoo Groups service (http://dir.groups.yahoo.com/dir/Music). This free, ad-supported service lets anyone create a "group" with an e-mail list, message archives, and the ability to share files and photos. With over 200,000 groups dealing with music the problem becomes one of choosing. There are scores, if not hundreds of groups devoted to particular genres. Popular artists can be counted on to have at least five groups devoted to them.

Figure 25.1. Yahoo Groups devoted to Baroque Music

Yahoo! Groups

Top > Music > Genres > Classical > **Baroque**

Group Listings

1 - 10 of 29 | **Previous | Next** [First | Last]

1 **handel-l**
HANDEL-L is a discussion list initially founded by The American Handel Society, but open to everybody wishing to discuss the music, life and times of George Frideric Handel (1685-1759), ... **more**
Members: 534 | Archives: Members only

2 **baroquemusiclovers**
Let's trade messages about recordings, concerts, performance practice, etc. regarding classical music from 1600 to 1750.
Members: 149 | Archives: Public

3 **Castrati_History**
Church and operatic castrati from an historian's point of view. This says it all, really; it would be very pleasant for us to continue sharing our sources of information, as we already ... **more**
Members: 145 | Archives: Members only

4 **ItalianBaroque**
A group dedicated to the discussion of recordings, composers, and history of Italian Baroque music. (picture : Benedetto Marcello)
Members: 100 | Archives: Members only

5 **Henry_Purcell**
For lovers of the English Orpheus - Henry Purcell. Discuss his art, his life and recordings and performances of Purcell's music.
Members: 63 | Archives: Members only

6 **Gluck**
For the discussion of the life, times, and music of Christoph Willibald Ritter von Gluck (1714-1787), one of the greatest and certainly the most undervalued composer of opera in the ... **more**
Members: 59 | Archives: Members only

There are two ways to find music groups on Yahoo. One is to browse the music group category listings (http://dir.groups.yahoo.com/dir/Music). The other is to do a keyword search. The advantage of using the categorized listings is that for each category you get a list of groups sorted by size. The group with the largest number of members is first, followed by the group with the next largest number of members, and so on. This is useful for narrowing down your choices when confronted with a large number of groups (e.g., 200+ groups listed in the Elvis Presley category). The advantage of a keyword search is that it may turn up relevant groups that haven't been filed under the expected category or for which a category doesn't exist.

If you are faced with lots of choices, use the following criteria to help you choose.

- **How many members are there?**
  Groups with more members tend to have more traffic and are more likely to be forums where your questions can be answered.

- **How much traffic is there?**
  A group's home page will tell you how many messages have been posted, by month, for the past couple of years. These numbers will tell you how active a group is, or if a group is dormant or abandoned.

- **Does the group have message archives?**
  A message archive lets you tap into the information shared in previous discussions and see if your question has already been answered. Sometimes these archives are only available to group members.

- **Of what quality are the message postings?**
  Scan the group's message archive, if it exists, and read a few messages. Then see what proportion of these messages contain relevant discussions. Geeks refer to this as the signal-to-noise ratio. Rambling off-topic discussions, contentious "flame wars," and spam all lower the signal-to-noise ratio and make a group less useful.

- **Is the group moderated?**
  Are there moderators or "list moms" policing the list and making sure that messages are "on topic." Though not all moderation is benign, it's nice to know that someone cares enough to do it. Moderated groups are also less likely to be plagued by spam.

Music Service Discussion Groups

Message boards provided by Internet music services can be useful. Examples include:

- **LAUNCHcast**
  The LAUNCHcast User Group (http://groups.yahoo.com/group/LAUNCHcast) lets users exchange tips and discuss music. Members also discuss new feature possibilities with the product manager. This group is moderated. Artist pages on LAUNCHcast also have a "communities" link that links to message boards and related Yahoo Groups.

- **eMusic**
  Users discuss music on genre specific message boards with an emphasis on the music available from eMusic. A generic message board is also available to discuss other issues and concerns. You don't have to subscribe to be able to access them. (http://msg.emusic.com/emusic/listnews)

- **Live365**
  Live365 broadcasters and listeners share information about music and radio stations available on Live365. Many Live365 stations have their own mailing lists or discussion groups, which you can find out about on the broadcaster's Web site. Many are Yahoo Groups.

Other Places to Look for Music Discussion Groups

- **MSN Groups** - http://groups.msn.com/browse.msnw?catid=50
  Similar to Yahoo Groups in function—just not as big. Run by Microsoft as part of its MSN service.

- **Catalist** - http://www.lsoft.com/lists/listref.html
  A directory of 75,000+ public mailing lists that use Listserv software.

- **Topica** - http://www.topica.com/dir/?cid=156
  Another service which hosts free e-mail discussion groups. Smaller than the Yahoo and MSN offerings.

- **Fan Web sites**
  Here, you can often find mailing lists or message boards for a particular artist. See Chapter 23, *Behind the Music: Questions About Artists*, for more information on fan Web sites.

Tips for Using Online Discussion Groups

- **Get the lay of the land before plunging in**
  Read whatever guidelines are posted for a group before posting messages. If an FAQ is available, read that as well. Then "lurk" for a bit—monitoring messages to get a feel for the group. If a message archive exists, search it to see if your question has already been answered.

- **Understand Netiquette**
  "Netiquette" refers to etiquette on the Internet—widely accepted norms for how to behave online. Web sites with Netiquette information can be found at: http://directory.google.com/Top/Computers/Internet/Etiquette.

- **Manage your e-mail**
  E-mail from discussion groups can overwhelm your inbox unless you take measures to control it. Using your mail reader to route discussion group messages to a designated folder is one good step. Another option is to request mailings in "digest" form, in which multiple postings (usually a day's worth) are combined into a single message.

Part Three

Internet Music Discovery Plans

26

An Internet Music Discovery Plan

After reading about the services discussed in this book, you may be asking yourself, "Where do I start?" and "What do I do next?" This part of the book attempts to answer that question. In Part One, you learned about the different types of online music services and what they can do for you. But reading about the services can only take you so far. To truly understand, you need to use them.

The following chapters contain concrete, seven-day plans for getting up-to-speed with key services and using them for music discovery. Your commitment is to spend a minimum of thirty minutes per day using the services. Your payoff will be increased music enjoyment and steady progress towards becoming a savvy user of these services.

What I suggest is that you spend time using at least one service of each type: an Internet radio service, a personalized radio service, an online jukebox service, and a downloading service. Pick the ones that most interesting to you and try them.

Internet Radio Service

- Live365 (Chapter 27)
- MSN Radio (Chapter 28)
- Musicmatch Online (Chapter 33)

Personalized Radio Service

- LAUNCHcast (Chapter 29)

Online Jukebox Service

- Rhapsody (Chapter 30)
- Musicmatch Online (Chapter 33)

Downloading Service
- iTunes Music Store - Download Store (Chapter 31)
- eMusic - Subscription-based service (Chapter 32)
- Musicmatch Online (Chapter 33)

Before Starting

Read the chapter in Part One that profiles the service, and make sure that your computer meets the minimum requirements for using the service. This information can be found in the *Getting Started* section of each chapter. Remember that no one service can do it all. I find that a combination of services works best. By trying multiple services, you will get a better understanding of the features and capabilities that will maximize your music enjoyment.

Although these plans are designed to take place over seven days, it is better to think of them as seven sessions. You can do them in less than seven days, or in more than seven days. In the case of fee-based services that provide seven-day free trials, you will want to complete the plan before the trial is up so as to avoid incurring charges.

Good luck and happy exploring!

27

Live365 Discovery Plan

What follows is a seven-day plan for getting up-to-speed with Live365 and putting its features to use. For background information on Live365, consult Chapter 2, *Live365: The Place to Start.*

Day 1

1. Go to the Live365 Web site (http://www.live365.com) and use the SIGN UP link to register as a user. Then download and configure a player. If you are a Windows user, select the *Player365* option. If you are a Macintosh user, select the *iTunes* option.

2. Select the LISTEN tab on Live365 home page and then browse the available stations by category. One good option is to select the EDITOR'S PICKS category. Station listings are sorted in order of popularity (by default), as measured by Total Listener Hours (TLH) in the last month.

3. Pick an interesting sounding station and click on the ◀ play button just to the left of the station name. Listen to the station for at least fifteen minutes. Repeat the process with a different station. If you like a station, add it to your MY PRESETS list, so you can return to it later. This can be done on the Live365 player by clicking on the ⊞ button next to where it says, ADD THIS STATION TO MY PRESETS. The option of clicking on this button is also available on directory listings and on station information Web pages. Building a good presets list is key to getting the most out of Live365.

4. While you are listening, take note of the playlist information that is displayed: song title, artist name, and CD title. If you come across a good song you never heard of before, click on the ⊞ icon to the right of the song display to add it to your Live365 WISHLIST, thus capturing the song information for future reference. If you click on the "thumbs up" icon, you'll be letting the broadcaster know that you like the track. Clicking "thumbs down" will do the opposite. The Live365 player also has a RATE THIS STATION menu that lets you rate the station on a scale from one (poor) to five (exceptional).

Note: If you run into problems, consult the help pages—which contain an FAQ and knowledge-base—or contact Live365's support personnel. As of this writing, there is a SUPPORT link available just underneath the COMMUNITY tab on the home page. To see it, you must click on the COMMUNITY tab.

Day 2

1. Find a new station to listen to. Listen to it for at least half an hour (unless you dislike it in which case feel free to find another). Each time you hear a new song that particularly interests you, add it your WISHLIST by clicking on the ⊞ icon next to the song title in the playlist display.

2. While you are listening, use the Live365 directory to find promising stations to add to your MY PRESETS list. Select the LISTEN tab on the home page, and then go to the FIND YOUR MUSIC section on the right side of the page. In addition to using the BROWSE menu, try the following techniques:

   • Do keyword searches using the supplied search box. This will help you find kinds of music not listed in the pull down genre menu. Examples of keywords that will pull up stations: bagpipes, wedding, polkas, Moroccan, barbershop. Be creative!

   • Use the ADVANCED SEARCH bar to do a keyword search against a category of stations. This gives you a more targeted search. For example, search for the keyword "blues" in the category of EDITORS PICKS stations to find blues stations that the Live365 editors approve of. To access the ADVANCED SEARCH bar, click on the word ADVANCED right next to the main search box.

   • Use the ADVANCED SEARCH bar to search for stations whose playlists carry a particular artist, track, or album. One of the pull-down menus lets you restrict the search to artists or albums or track names. This lets you find stations that play specific music you are interested in.

   Note: Use the sorting options to help you with large listings. You can sort your station listings by clicking on the column headings. Click on the TLH heading to sort listings by Total Listener Hours (in the past 30 days). Click on the SPEED heading to sort station listings by connection speed. Clicking again on either listing will reverse the sort order.

3. As you find interesting stations add them to your MY PRESETS list. If a station doesn't pan out you can always remove it from the list. Your MY PRESETS list can be accessed from your MYLIVE365 page.

4. Make sure to try stations which play music you've never heard of or know little about—it'll expand your horizons!

Optional

- For a taste of what ad-free access to Live365 is like, sign up for a free trial of Live365's *VIP Preferred Listener* subscription plan. As of this writing, a five-day free trial is available.

- Thousands of Live365 stations are only available to *Preferred Listener* subscribers. Now is your chance to try some of them.

- The Preferred Listener plan also allows you to use Live365's premium *Radio365* player software, available to both Windows and Macintosh users. Use of this player is not covered in this chapter; for the purposes of music discovery the free player options are just as good. Macintosh users should be aware that the Mac version of *Radio365* has a direct link to the iTunes Music Store, allowing you to buy tracks that you hear on Live365. If you are interested in using the iTunes Music Store, you are recommended to give this a try.

- If you don't wish to become a paying customer, make sure to cancel before the trial is over. Put a reminder in your calendar to make sure you do this.

Day 3

1. Listen to a new station for at least half an hour.

2. While you are listening, go to your WISHLIST page. You can do this by clicking on the WISHLIST tab on your MYLIVE365 page. MYLIVE365

3. Review your WISHLIST, and take note of the tracks that you have added. If you haven't yet added any, add a couple from the current broadcast you are listening to. This information can help you explore new music of interest to you. With it you can:

   - Click on the BUY button to execute a search of Amazon.com's site using information about that CD. If the CD is available there, you can buy it or read customer reviews of it, assuming reviews are available. Sometimes you'll get useful information. Other times you won't.

   - Click on either the track, artist, or album names for a given track and you will be provided with a list of Live365 stations whose current playlists include that track, artist, or album name. This will help you identify other stations to try.

   - Open up a new Web browser window and search for information about the CDs or artists captured on your WISHLIST. Part Two, *Music Information Services*, describes useful Web sites that you can use to find album reviews, artist information, and more.

   - When you are done using information on your WISHLIST, you have the option of deleting it.

Day 4

1. Listen to a new station for at least half an hour.

2. While you are listening, take the time to learn more about the stations you have been listening to. Go to your MY PRESETS page and click on the station name for a few of your favorite stations. In each case, this will take you to the station's Web page on Live365. Review the information that is there:

   - Sample tracks listing

   - Broadcaster's comments

   - Connection speed

   - Total listener hours (in past 30 days)

   - Listener rating of station

   - Other Live365 stations this broadcaster recommends

3. In the upper right hand corner of most Live365 station pages there is a link for the BROADCASTER'S WEB SITE. Click on this. This will take you to an external Web site that will often provide more detailed information about the station. This can include station news, free downloads, merchandise, newsletter information, and more.

4. Each station page also has a BROADCASTER'S PROFILE tab. Clicking on this will provide a link to a profile. Some of these contain interesting information. Many do not.

5. Repeat this process for any Live365 station that you listen to regularly.

Day 5

1. Listen to a new station for at least half an hour.

2. While you are listening, go to your MY LIVE365 page and select the AD-VANCED SETTINGS tab, which allows you to customize the display of station listings.

3. The default setting is to show all the information for a radio station, with listings sorted in order of descending popularity as measured by Total-Listening-Hours (TLH) in the past thirty days. Each page contains twenty-five listings. To get more listings, click on the NEXT PAGE link. These settings may be fine for you, but you should know how to change them. Options include:

   - Changing the display of Total-Listening-Hours (TLH) and Station Ratings to use text numerical displays rather than icons (e.g., 5,572 vs. three "listener" icons for Total-Listening-Hours).

   - Change the default sort order of the station listings (e.g., sort by station name rather than by TLH rankings).

   - Change the number of listings displayed on one page from the default setting of twenty-five. If you'd rather scroll down a long list than click NEXT (page) a bunch of times, then you'll want to increase this number.

   - Change the information that gets displayed for each station. By cutting this back, I've made it so that each listing takes up less space. By doing this and increasing the number of listings displayed per page to a hundred or more, I've made it so that I can quickly scan my entire presets list (all 88 of them) on one page.

   As an example, these are my preferred settings:

   - Text display for both Total-Listening-Hours and STATION RATINGS

   - Sort by STATION TITLE (ascending)

   - Listings displayed per page: 100

   - Fields removed from display: NUMBER, BROADCASTER NAME, DESCRIPTION, and PROFILE (If I want details I can go to the station page)

Day 6

1. Today let Live365 pick some stations for you. Go to your MYLIVE365 page and turn your attention to the FIND YOUR MUSIC menu on the right side of the page. Using the BROWSE pull-down menu, pick any category with the exception of MY PRESETS or MY RECOMMENDATIONS: it could be ALL BROAD-CASTS, EDITOR'S PICKS or a genre category (e.g., WORLD). Once a list of stations has been displayed go to the top of the list and hit the PLAY RANDOM button, which should be clearly visible. A station will then be randomly selected from the list and launched in your player. Don't like it? Click on the PLAY RANDOM button again. This is great for all you channel flippers out there.

2. Listen to at least three different stations for a total of thirty minutes. While you're listening, check out the station information Web pages, and if available, the broadcaster Web sites. If you like a station, add it to your presets list.

Optional

-   If you signed up for a trial of the VIP Preferred Listener plan, remember to cancel it if you are not interested in becoming a paying subscriber.

Day 7

1. Listen to a new station for at least half an hour.

2. It's time to anoint a favorite station. At the top of your MY PRESETS lists is a place to designate your FAVORITE STATION. This puts the station front and center, making it easy to play it in the future. Also, by doing this, you give the broadcaster some recognition, and in some cases, make him or her eligible for cash payments from Live365.

Live 365 Summary

Having completed the steps outlined you should now:

- Understand the richness of programming that Live365 has to offer.

- Have a collection of preset stations you can quickly access.

- Understand how to use the playlist information and other features on the Live365 player.

- Be able to effectively navigate the Live365 directory to find new and interesting radio stations.

- Be able to use the WISHLIST feature to track new artists, CDs, and songs of interest, and be able to use it to find more information about the music, and if you desire, buy it.

- Be able to customize your station display listings and use the PLAY RANDOM feature.

- Be aware of the Live365 Preferred Listener fee-based offering, and of the different subscription options.

28

MSN Radio Discovery Plan

What follows is a seven-day plan for getting started with MSN Radio. For background on MSN Radio, consult Chapter 3, *MSN Radio: A Toolbox for Music Exploration.*

Day 1

1. Go the MSN Radio Web page (http://entertainment.msn.com/stations) and sign-up for a free trial of MSN Radio Plus, which as of this writing is one month long. You will get a login ID and password. If you already have a Microsoft Passport ID, this will be your ID. You will be required to supply your credit card information. Mark down the trial expiration date on your calendar. You'll need to cancel by this date to avoid incurring charges.

2. Browse the available stations using the MSN Radio Web page, pick one of interest and start playing it. Enter your ID and password when prompted. Note that most of the stations have a plus icon next to them, which means they are only available to MSN Radio Plus subscribers. Listen for thirty minutes, while taking the time to try the different controls on the player: pause, skip to next song, control volume (including mute), adjust sound quality, and rate music.

3. Click where it says ADD STATION TO FAVORITES. A separate Web browser window will open, showing your FAVORITE STATIONS list containing the station you just added. Bookmark this FAVORITE STATIONS page using your Web browser.

4. While you are listening, take the time to read all the descriptions of the STYLE radio stations, starting with the ALTERNATIVE category and proceeding through the WORLD category. To do this, you will need to click on each category link separately. This will give you a full sense of the richness of MSN Radio's music style offerings.

Day 2

1. Return to the FAVORITE STATIONS page that you bookmarked last time. Click on the name of the station you saved. This will load the station and it will begin to play.

2. Now click on the RADIO TUNER button on the player. Follow the steps provided in the tuner window and pick a new station to listen to. Listen for at least fifteen minutes. If you like the station, click on the ADD STATION TO FAVORITES link.

3. While you are listening, take note of the artist names that get displayed in the NOW PLAYING display area of the player. When you see one you haven't heard of before, or whose sound interests you, click on the artist name. This will load a separate browser window with an artist information page.

4. Scan this page and take note of the different sections, and the information that is provided. Read the artist biography, then see what albums this artist has released. Click on one of the album names. If you see a review of this album available, read it.

5. For most, if not all artists, there is the option to play a "SoundsLike" station for that artist. If you see the option, click on the link to play the station. Listen to it for at least fifteen minutes. If you like the station, click on the ADD STATION TO FAVORITES link.

Day 3

1. Return to the MSN Radio stations Web page and pick a new station, preferably in a new category, and listen to it for at least fifteen minutes. If you like it, click on the ADD STATION TO FAVORITES link.

2. While you are listening, take note of the song and album names that get displayed in the NOW PLAYING display area in the player. When you hear a song that interests you, click on the album name. This will load a separate browser window with an album information page.

3. Look for the song listing. When you find the song that is playing, click on the EXPAND/COLLAPSE icon to the right of the song title. This will open up a song information menu. Note the available options. These can include the following: PLAY A SOUNDSLIKE STATION (based on the song), VIEW A SOUNDSLIKE SONG LIST, PLAY A CLIP, ADD TO FAVORITES, and RATE THE SONG. If you have the option, try playing a SoundsLike station based on the song. Listen to it for at least fifteen minutes. See if you can detect similarities between the original song and what gets played on this station. If you like the station, click on the ADD STATION TO FAVORITES link.

4. While you continue to listen, see if there is a review available on the album information page. If there is, read it.

Optional

- Use the SEARCH BY SONG option on the MSN Radio Web page to see if you can find a favorite song of yours. If you can find it, see if there is an option to play a SoundsLike station based on the song. If so, play it and see what gets played. If not, try again with another song that you know. If you like the station, click on the ADD STATION TO FAVORITES link.

Day 4

1. Return to the MSN Radio stations Web page and pick a new station, in a new category, and listen to it for at least fifteen minutes. If you like it, click on the ADD STATION TO FAVORITES link.

2. Click on an artist name in the NOW PLAYING display to load an artist information page for that artist. Scroll down and look for the heading, near the bottom, that reads RELATED MUSIC STYLES AND STATIONS. When you have found it, look for the STYLES that are listed and click on one of the links given. This will load a style information page in your browser window.

3. Read the description of the style, and scan the given lists of IMPORTANT ALBUMS, KEY ARTISTS, and RECOMMENDED RADIO stations. Try one of the radio stations listed here. Listen for at least fifteen minutes. If you like this station, make sure to click on the ADD STATION TO FAVORITES link.

Optional

- If more than one style is listed on the artist information page, then click on a second style name and repeat step three.

Day 5

1. Return to the MSN Radio stations Web page and pick a new station, this time from one of the following theme categories: LET'S EAT, LET'S DRINK, or WORKOUT MUSIC. Listen to it for at least fifteen minutes. Then pick another station from these categories and listen to it for fifteen minutes.

2. While you are listening to these stations, go back to the MSN Radio stations Web page and take the time to read all the descriptions of the MOOD & THEME STATIONS. To do this, you will need to click on each category link separately. If you like any of these stations, remember to click on the ADD STATION TO FAVORITES link.

3. If you hear any songs of interest, click on the song name, go to the album page, locate the song name, and then click on the ADD THIS SONG TO MY FAVORITES link.

Day 6

1. Return to the MSN Radio stations Web page and pick a new station, this time from one of the following two categories: FOR THE WORKPLACE or ALL DAY MUSIC. Pick a station that you might like to use for background music, something that doesn't demand much of your attention, but that looks different than music you are used to. Play this station for at least fifteen minutes. Then pick another station from one of these categories and play it for fifteen minutes.

2. While these stations are playing, do something else on (or near) your computer. If you can do work from home, by all means do some work. Compose an e-mail to a colleague. Or write a letter to a friend. Balance your checkbook. Surf the Web. Something that demands some attention.

3. When the experience is over, ask yourself whether stations like these might have a place in your work day.

Alternative

- If the thought of easy listening music is a turnoff for you, even if it is light years from the Muzak of old, break out the exercise mat and try HEART RATE RADIO. Do some crunches, jumping jacks, or whatever it is you do for exercise indoors.

Day 7

1. Start up the MSN Radio player, and start playing the first station that comes to mind. Listen for at least fifteen minutes.

2. Go to your MSN MY FAVORITES page (http://entertainment.msn.com/user) and review the artists, albums, songs, and stations you have saved thus far. This page will display the two most recently added "favorite" artists, albums, songs, and stations, along with links to the complete "all your favorites" lists in each category. Follow these links to see the full favorites lists. Here is where you can delete entries. Simply click on the EXPAND/COLLAPSE icon to the right of the listed "favorite." This will open up a menu, giving you the option to delete the entry.

   Unfortunately, MSN has not made it very easy to get to these Web pages. Therefore, you should consider bookmarking these pages with your Web browser, so that you can return to them easily.

3. Now find a new station you haven't tried yet, and listen to it for at least fifteen minutes. If you haven't yet, consider trying one of the Grammy Award Winner or Celebrity DJ stations.

MSN Radio Summary

Having completed the steps outlined you should now:

- Be familiar with the full range of MSN Radio's available radio stations.

- Know how to play SoundsLike radio stations based on a given song, album, or artist. This includes knowing how to access SoundsLike lists of songs, albums, and artists.

- Know how to access artist information, album reviews, and music genre information using MSN's music information links.

- Know how to create and use MY FAVORITES lists of songs, albums, artists, and radio stations.

- Know how to use the radio tuner and other player controls.

29

LAUNCHcast Discovery Plan

What follows is a seven-day plan for getting up-to-speed with LAUNCHcast and putting its features to use. For background information on LAUNCHcast, consult Chapter 6, *LAUNCHcast: Your Own Personal Station.*

Day 1

1. Go to Yahoo's LAUNCHcast Web site (http://radio.yahoo.com) and sign up for the free version of LAUNCHcast's service. A Yahoo ID and password is required to the use the service. If you already have one you can use that. If you don't, you'll need to sign up to get one. Note that this ID can be used for other Yahoo services. To automate login in the future, you'll want to check the option that says, REMEMBER MY ID ON THIS COMPUTER.

2. You will be prompted for some music preference information to get things started. Supply this information and then play your station for at least thirty minutes. While you are listening, use the rating controls on the player to rate each song on a scale from zero stars (never play this again) to four stars (can't get enough). For songs you never want to hear again, click on the ban symbol—a circle with a red line through it. You will never hear it again. There is also a separate skip button. You're in the driver's seat now!

   At the same time you have the option of rating albums and artists too, by selecting the appropriate control on the player. Don't despair if you're getting lots of music you don't like. Diligent use of the rating tool will ensure that your station gets better as your music ratings accumulate. Seeing your station take shape and get better over time can be quite satisfying. Once your profile starts consistently producing music that you like, you won't be as compelled to rate everything that you hear. For now, though, you should be rating a lot of music.

3. While you are listening, go to the LAUNCHcast help page and read the section titled RATING MUSIC so that you can better understand how the process works.

4. Find the link just above the rating controls which says MY STATION. Click on this link to be taken to your MY STATION Web page. On the left hand side of this page there is a menu. Find the EDIT—GENRES link and click on it. Now rate all the genres according to how much you want them to play. For most of the main genre categories there are subgenres (e.g., under Jazz there is Latin Jazz, Big Band Jazz, and other categories). I recommend rating all subgenres to exercise maximum control over your playlist. To access these, simply click on the EDIT SUBGENRES links.

5. If the player doesn't seem to be working properly, check the help files, and contact Yahoo support if necessary. *Note:* The only way I have been able to find a link to their support people is within the LAUNCHcast frequently asked questions (FAQ) list. At the bottom of each question and answer is a question to the reader, "Is this enough information?" If you click the NO button, you will be taken to a form for contacting Yahoo customer support.

Day 2

1. Start up your station and listen for at least thirty minutes, rating music as you hear it. If you miss rating a song before it ends you can access a Web page listing recently played songs and rate (or re-rate) songs that have played during your current session. The link to this page can be located on the player by clicking on the left or right arrows located at the bottom of the SONG INFO window. Repeatedly clicking on either arrow will cycle the display through a series of links. Try it. One of these links is titled HISTORY: VIEW A LIST OF SONGS YOU'VE HEARD RECENTLY. Click on it to access a Web page showing your recently played songs.

2. Now it's time to make sure that key bands and artists get included in your station profile. Go to your MY STATION Web page and use the provided search box to search for artists you want added to your station. When you find the artist, go to their artist page and use the RATE THIS ARTIST selector to rate the artist highly. Check the discography for albums that have the LAUNCHcast player icon next to them. These are the ones that can be played on your station. If you know something about the albums, rate them too. Click on an album name, and you'll be taken to the album information Web page. From here you can rate individual songs. Any truly favorite songs? Rate them highly to make sure they get airplay.

Optional

• A LAUNCHcast user has created a Web page that lists artists available in each genre and subgenre. This is an unofficial, work-in-progress, but you might find it helpful in deciding which artists to add to your station. It also provides insight into how artists are categorized. As of this writing, it can be found at: http://www.launchinfo.org.

Day 3

1. Start up your station and listen to it for at least fifteen minutes, rating music as you hear it.

2. When you hear an interesting song, go to the song display on your LAUNCHcast player and click on the artist name (it's also possible to click on the song or album name). A Web browser window will open showing the artist information Web page.

3. Explore the artist information available from the menu on the left side of this Web page. What's available varies with the popularity of the artist, but can include news, photos, videos, reviews, interviews, Web links and a brief biography. Browse some of this information.

4. On this same artist Web page you should be able to find—for most artists available on LAUNCHcast—a fan station. A fan station plays music highly rated by LAUNCHcast users who also like this artist. Play the station for at least fifteen minutes, rating music as you hear it. *Note:* So long as you are logged in, ratings made while listening to *any* LAUNCHcast station will be added to your profile.

Day 4

1. Start up your LAUNCHcast player and use the STATION DIRECTORY tab at the top of the player window to browse the available pre-programmed stations. Select one and listen to it for at least fifteen minutes. If you hear music that you want to include or exclude from your personal station, rate it accordingly. Consider the pre-programmed stations as alternatives to your personal station: something to listen to when you're in the mood for a specific kind of music.

2. While listening, return to your MY STATION Web page. Scan down the page to where it says RATINGS LEVEL. Are you a NEWBIE, LISTENER, or an ENTHU- SIAST? One of your goals should be to rate at least 100 songs—and attain at least a LISTENER rating—before you are done with day seven of this plan. Now go to the left column and click on the link that says EDIT, which will load the EDIT MY STATION Web page. Review your genre, artist, album, and song ratings lists and make any changes you deem necessary. Note that ratings can be changed. This way you can control play frequency over time. You can also create an ABOUT MY STATION message. Visible to anybody who sees your station Web page, this message lets you tell prospective listeners what your station is all about.

Optional

- For a taste of what ad-free access to LAUNCHcast is like, sign up for a free trial of LAUNCHcast Plus. As of this writing, LAUNCHcast is offering a 7-day free trial of the service, which requires that you supply them with credit card information.

- LAUNCHcast plus adds more pre-programmed radio stations and two new capabilities as well: Moods, where you can create substations that provide genre specific slices of your personal station; and the ability to "subscribe" to other listener stations and allow their profiles to influence the music that is served to you. Stations so chosen become identified as "influencers." See the LAUNCHcast FAQ—accessible from the help page— for more information.

- To avoid inadvertently activating a paying subscription, mark down the trial expiration date on your calendar and cancel the subscription before the trial expires.

Day 5

1. Start up your station and listen for at least thirty minutes, rating music as you hear it.

2. While you are listening, check out the LAUNCHcast User Group Web page: http://groups.yahoo.com/group/launchcast. Here you can learn more about the LAUNCHcast User Group, and join the group if you are interested. Once you've joined you can access a searchable archive of messages and choose whether to receive message postings via e-mail.

3. Now try and think of specific albums that you would like to hear on LAUNCHcast. Have any of your favorite artists released an album lately? Are there some old favorites you would like included in your station's program? With any luck, you can think of at least one album. Go to your MY STATION Web page and use the provided search box to search for the albums you want added to your station. If you find that an album is available, rate it highly (four stars). Then wait for songs from the album to start appearing on your station. If, after a while, you want the album to play less frequently, then go back and lower the album rating.

4. Before you finish for the day, click on the HELP & OPTIONS tab on the player. Take a look at the available options. Clicking on the CUSTOMIZE MY STATION option will take you to the EDIT MY STATION Web page. Clicking on the EDIT EXPLICIT LYRICS link takes you to a Web page where you can block songs with explicit lyrics from appearing on your station. The SHARE MY STATION link takes you to a Web form will allows you to e-mail information about your station to friends.

   The EDIT RATING SCALE preference allows you to select an advanced 0-to-100 rating scale, to use instead of the default star rating scheme for rating music. This 0-to-100 was the original scheme that LAUNCHcast used, is favored by many of LAUNCHcast's original users, including the control freaks among us.

Day 6

1. Today's task is to explore personal stations created by other LAUNCHcast users. Start up your station and start listening. When you hear a song you like, click on the song name in your player window. This will take you to a Web page for that song. A short way down the page should be a heading that reads FANS OF THIS SONG. Below this is a list of LAUNCHcast users that have rated this song highly.

2. Next to each user ID, there are two buttons that read: LISTEN and INFO. Pick a user on the list and click on the INFO button next to their listing. This will take you to the station information page for that person. Take a look at their station and the music they have rated. If it interests you, play it for fifteen minutes—rating any music that you hear. If not, try looking at another station. Or use the artist pages to find fans of another song, album, or artist. Then listen to a station and rate music that you hear. If you really like it, and are a LAUNCHcast Plus user, you have the option of "subscribing" to that station. To do this, go to the station information page and click on the SUBSCRIBE TO MY TASTES button.

Optional

- Note that you have the option of rating any albums, artists, or songs that you see on another listener's rating pages. So if you recognize music that you want added or banned from your station profile, this is an opportunity to rate it accordingly.

Day 7

1. Start up your station and listen for at least thirty minutes, rating music as you hear it.

2. With any luck, by now you've rated more than 100 songs and your Station Rating level has risen above that of "Newbie." If not, keep at it. With time, your station will develop into something truly personal.

Optional

- If you use Yahoo's instant messenger software, consider using their latest version, which allows you to access LAUNCHcast controls from within Yahoo Messenger. Here, you also have the option of displaying the currently playing song next to your status line so that other Yahoo Messenger users can see what you're listening to.

LAUNCHcast Summary

Having completed the steps outlined you should now:

- Be able to rate music while listening to it and also by using the genre, artist, album, and song pages on the LAUNCHcast Web site.

- Be able to use all player controls.

- Be able to find artist information Web pages on the LAUNCHcast Web site and use them to learn more about the artists.

- Be able to find and play fan stations, pre-programmed stations, and stations created by other LAUNCHcast users.

- Be able to edit your station and share it with others.

- Know what the LAUNCHcast User Group is and what it has to offer.

- Understand the LAUNCHcast Plus subscription option.

30

Rhapsody Discovery Plan

What follows is a seven-day plan for getting up-to-speed with Rhapsody and putting its features to use. For background information on Rhapsody, consult Chapter 9, *Rhapsody: A Near-Celestial Jukebox*.

Day 1

1. Go to the Rhapsody Web site (http://www.rhapsody.com) and sign up for a free trial of Rhapsody's All-Access subscription program and download their player software. To avoid inadvertently activating a paying subscription, mark down the trial expiration date on your calendar and cancel the subscription before the trial expires.

2. Start up the player. Go to the HELP menu and click on the TECHNICAL SUPPORT option. Now click on the link that says TOUR RHAPSODY to see a brief, helpful presentation on the different features available in Rhapsody. The presentation will take approximately two minutes.

3. Now return to the player and use the SEARCH box to locate some of your favorite artists and albums. When you find an album or track that interests you, click on the SAVE TO LIBRARY icon next to the album or track name. This will place the album or track into your MY LIBRARY collection of saved music, from which it can be accessed in the future. To play an album or track, you can either click on the PLAY NOW icon, or use your mouse to drag the album or track from your MY LIBRARY collection into the playlist window. Double-clicking on the first track on the playlist will start playback.

4. Find one or more albums that you love and play them. Experiment with the playlist window to see what you can do with it. See if you can add individual tracks from other albums, reorder the playlist, and delete tracks.

Day 2

1. Start up your player. Go to the BROWSE GENRES menu on the left hand side of the music information window and click on one of the genre category links (e.g., JAZZ). This will take you to the home page for that genre and reveal a SUBGENRES menu, also located on the left hand side of the window. Clicking on one of these links (e.g., ACID JAZZ) will take you to a home page for that subgenre. Find a genre or subgenre page for a type of music you are unfamiliar with.

2. Play the genre sampler playlist that appears in the center of the music information window.

3. While you are listening to the sampler, scan the lists of MOST POPULAR ARTISTS and KEY ARTISTS. Also click on the CHARTS link to see what tracks and albums are popular with other Rhapsody users. If an album or track catches your interest, click on the SAVE TO LIBRARY icon to add it your library. Note that some artists are filed under multiple genres and styles, and links to these genres can be found at the bottom of the artist page. Clicking on these genre links will take you to the appropriate genre pages.

4. To find out more about an album, click on the BUY CDS link, which will launch a Web browser window and take you to the Amazon.com Web site. Here you can read album reviews (if available). Alternately, you can open up a separate Web browser window and go to the Allmusic Web site (http://www.allmusic.com), where you can search by artist or album. If you're interested in the song that is currently playing, you can click on the ALBUM INFO button on the player to pull up the album information page.

5. Play another album.

Day 3

1. Today's task is to create and save a music mix. Start up your player and press the CLEAR button at the bottom of your playlist window. This will clear any tracks left over from your previous session.

2. Think of playlist or music mix you'd like to create. It could be a collection of favorite tracks or a thematic mix (workout music, best songs from a particular artist, etc.). With over 740,000 tracks to choose from, you've got options! Be creative.

3. To include tracks from your library collection simply drag them into the playlist window. To include other tracks not already in your library, use the Rhapsody search tool to find them. You can then add these tracks to your library and then drag them to your playlist, or simply click on the PLAY NOW icon, which will also add them to the playlist.

   Note: You can change the settings on your player so that clicking PLAY NOW simply adds the track to your playlist but doesn't play it immediately. This prevents interruptions to music that is currently playing. A MY LIBRARY setting also controls what happens when you double-click on a track in your library. Is the track just added to the bottom of the playlist, or is it added and then immediately played? My preference is for the latter. Go to the OPTIONS menu to change these settings.

4. When you are done with the playlist, click on the SAVE button and name it. It will now be stored in the PLAYLISTS category of your MY LIBRARY collection, from where you can retrieve it later to play or modify. Having friends who subscribe to Rhapsody makes it more fun—because you can click on the SEND button to e-mail the playlist to them. It's a good argument for nagging your friends to join.

Day 4

1. Use the SEARCH box or the BROWSE GENRE menu to find an artist who interests you—ideally one you don't know much about. Go to that artist's page and click on the PLAY SAMPLER NOW icon to load a sampler playlist. Now listen to it.

2. Look at the ALBUMS list on the left hand part of the music information window. At the top of the list there are two radio-button choices: AVAILABLE ONLY and VIEW ALL. Click on the VIEW ALL option. Now you are seeing a complete list of albums for this artist. Any grayed out titles are not available on Rhapsody. This is a good way assessing what's missing from the Rhapsody catalog. Other services don't give you this information.

3. Not sure which album to play first from this artist? Open up a Web browser and go to the Allmusic Web site (http://www.allmusic.com/) and read the reviews. For more information on how to find reviews, consult Chapter 18, *Finding Album Reviews*.

4. Pick an album and play it. If you like it, or don't have time to listen to it now—then save it to your library.

5. Explore some of the other information on the artist home page. Check out the MOST POPULAR TRACKS list, the list of SIMILAR ARTISTS, and the list of genres that the artist is FILED UNDER, located at the bottom of the page.

6. Now play the artist's radio station, also available on the artist page under the heading RADIO PLUS. The music you'll hear—which includes some music not available on-demand on Rhapsody—will come from related artists, as well as from the artist. Listen for at least fifteen minutes. Feel free to make liberal use of the skip button to sample more music. If you hear a song you like, click on the ALBUM INFO button to see if the track or album is available for on-demand access. If it is, then save the track or album to your MY LIBRARY collection.

Day 5

1. Start up your player and click on the RADIO button, located just to the left of the SEARCH box.

2. On the left side of the window there is a column labeled STATION GENRES. Click on the link just below it, which says SHOW ALL STATIONS. This will display an annotated list of all of Rhapsody's pre-programmed radio stations.

3. Now scroll through the list, looking at the station descriptions. Then pick one station and hit the PLAY button. If you find others that look interesting, click on the SAVE button, which will add them to the RADIO STATIONS category of your MY LIBRARY collection.

4. Listen to the radio station for at least fifteen minutes. If you hear a song you like, click on the ALBUM INFO button to see if the track or album can be saved to your MY LIBRARY collection. If you can, save it.

5. Now click on the RADIO Button again, to return to the Radio Home Page.

6. Turn your attention to the panel in the middle of the window, where it says, CREATE A CUSTOM STATION. Enter the names of up to five artists you are interested in hearing on your station (you'll have the opportunity to enter up to five more in a subsequent dialog box). Give the station a name, save it, and play it. Listen for at least fifteen minutes. Note that you will hear mostly "related" music on this station. If you hear a song you like, click on the ALBUM INFO button to see if the track or album can be saved to your MY LIBRARY collection. If you can, save it.

Day 6

1. Today it's time to investigate the CD burning feature on Rhapsody, which requires that you have a CD burner and blank CD-R or CD-R/W disks. To make music from Rhapsody portable, you need to use the CD Burning feature, and pay a per-track fee (currently $0.79 – charged to your credit card). Start up your player, pick a radio station, and start playing it.

2. First review the albums and tracks in your MY LIBRARY collection to see which tracks are available (licensed) for burning. Do this by clicking on the BURN CD tab right next to the MY LIBRARY tab. You will now see a view of your library that shows you which tracks are burnable. Any albums or tracks that are grayed out are *not* available for burning. The others are. Also, as you browse the catalog, note that albums and tracks that are burnable will have a flame icon next to them.

3. Drag any tracks you are interested in burning into the PLAYLIST window (now called the BURN LIST). You can save this as a playlist and burn it later, or just use it as a playlist. If you are ready to burn a disk, go ahead.

Day 7

1. Start up your player and turn your attention to the JUST ADDED ALBUMS listing in the music information window. Scan the list and play or save any albums that look interesting. Think of it like the new book cart at the library. You never know what you're going to find.

2. Click on the MORE link at the bottom of the list to see more newly added albums. Use the opportunity to find some music that's totally different from what you're used to. See what it does for you. If one doesn't do, try another. That's the beauty of Rhapsody: trying new music doesn't cost you anything extra. So do it. Expand your horizons!

3. Assuming you have completed this program in seven days and your free trial is about to expire, you need to cancel the subscription or let it become active. Do this by using the MANAGE MY ACCOUNT option on the MY ACCOUNT pull down menu at the top of the player. If you need more time to decide then cancel the trial now. You can sign up for a paying subscription later once you've made your decision.

Rhapsody Summary

Having completed the steps outlined you should now:

- Be able to navigate the Rhapsody catalog and find specific music that you are looking for.

- Be able to use Rhapsody to learn more about artists and music genres.

- Be able to use Rhapsody's radio service for music discovery.

- Be able to create and share playlists.

- Be able to burn CDs using Rhapsody.

- Have a Rhapsody Library of saved artists, albums, and playlists.

31

iTunes Music Store Discovery Plan

What follows is a seven-day plan for getting up-to-speed with the iTunes Music Store, putting its features to use, and learning how to use it for music discovery. For background information on this service, consult Chapter 11, *iTunes Music Store: Downloads for the iPod People*. In order to use the iTunes Music Store, you will need to download and install Apple's free *iTunes* jukebox software, which is available for Macintosh OS X and Windows XP/2000 users. The download URL is: http://www.apple.com/itunes/download.

Unlike the other fee-based services covered in this section, the iTunes Music Store offers no free trial. So pursuing this discovery plan will cost money. If you would like to try a downloading service without having to spend any money, then I recommend trying eMusic.

Day 1

1. Once you have downloaded the *iTunes* player, you will need to create an iTunes Music Store account. To do this, click on the ACCOUNT SIGN IN button (located in the upper right hand corner of the player) and then select the option to CREATE NEW ACCOUNT. You will then be asked to agree to Apple's terms and conditions statement, create a user ID, and supply your credit card information.

2. Before you buy any music, consider whether you want to use the one-click purchasing method or the shopping cart method. The one-click method is the default method. If you do nothing, this is the method that will be used. When you click the BUY button on an album or a track, the music is immediately downloaded and your credit card is charged.

   If you choose the shopping cart method, instead of seeing a BUY button associated with each album and track, you will see an ADD button. Clicking on this button will put music into your shopping cart. The downloading and charging process won't begin until you go into your shopping cart and click on the BUY NOW button. This method adds an extra step to the purchase process, but gives you extra time to reconsider your purchase decisions. It also separates the selection and final purchase decisions and lets you batch your purchases.

To enable this option, go to the EDIT menu and select PREFERENCES and then the STORE tab. From here you can select the BUY USING A SHOPPING CART option. It is just as easy to switch back and select the BUY AND DOWNLOAD USING 1-CLICK option.

3. Start up the *iTunes* jukebox player. Click on the MUSIC STORE icon in the left column. This will load the iTunes Music Store display in the main *iTunes* window. Now take a look at the NEW RELEASES section near the top of the page. You will see a row of album images, bracketed on either side with arrow icons. Clicking on these arrows will scroll the display to the right or left, bringing more albums into view. Click on one of the albums to see the purchase details. Note that you can use the back arrow on the player (located just to the left of the "home" icon) to return to the previous screen. Repeat the process for the other sections: EXCLUSIVES, PRE-RELEASES, JUST-ADDED, and STAFF FAVORITES.

4. Now click on the small "home" icon at the top of the page, to ensure that you are on the iTunes Music Store home page. Now review the TODAY'S TOPS SONGS and TODAY'S TOP ALBUMS lists. Click on the TOP 100 SONGS and TOP 100 ALBUMS links to see the entire lists. Buy or add to your shopping cart any songs or albums that you feel like buying.

Day 2

1. Start up the *iTunes* jukebox player. Instead of clicking on the MUSIC STORE icon, this time click on the RADIO icon just above it. Once you do this, the window to the right will be loaded with a menu of radio genre categories. Select a category of interest and double-click on it. This will open up a menu of radio stations for that category.

2. Choose a radio stream from the listing given and double-click on it to play the station. Listen to the station for at least fifteen minutes. See if the currently playing song is listed while the station is played. Some stations allow this, while others do not.

3. While you listen to the station, open up all the other categories and browse the selection of streams. This will give you an idea of the rich listening options that are available for free using the iTunes software. See Chapter 1, *Internet Radio: Leaving Your Home Town,* for more on how to get the most out of Internet radio.

4. Listen to another station for at least fifteen minutes.

   Note: You now have the option of listening to radio while you browse the iTunes Music Store. In the following days of this plan, consider starting up a radio station prior to beginning the steps for that day. If you have another Internet radio service that you prefer, use it instead.

Optional

- For Macintosh Users: Sign-up for a trial of Live365's Internet Radio service VIP Preferred Membership. Use the Macintosh version of the *Radio365* player, which gives you the option of buying tracks from the iTunes Music Store. See Chapter 2, *Live365: The Place to Start,* for more information.

Day 3

1. Start up the *iTunes* jukebox player. Click on the MUSIC STORE icon in the left column. Near the top left hand corner of the home page is a pull down menu, labeled CHOOSE GENRE. Click on it and select a genre of interest.

2. Browse the various sections (NEW RELEASES, STAFF FAVORITES, etc.) to see if you find any albums of interest. Likewise, check the TODAY'S TOP SONGS and TODAY'S TOP ALBUMS lists. Buy or add to your shopping cart any songs or albums that you feel like buying.

3. Try the same for another genre. This time, click on an album of interest, then click on the artist's name to load an artist information page. If this page has an artist biography, read it. If not, see if you can find another artist page that does have an artist biography available. Take note of the information provided for each artist (TOP DOWNLOADED SONGS, TOP DOWNLOADED ALBUMS, TOP RATED IMIXES, etc.). Buy or add to your shopping cart any songs or albums that you feel like buying.

Day 4

1. Start up the *iTunes* jukebox player. Click on the MUSIC STORE icon in the left column. Now have a look at the ITUNES ESSENTIALS section, which lists music playlists put together by the iTunes Music Store staff. You should see approximately ten playlists listed. If you click on either the ITUNES ESSENTIALS heading or the SEE ALL link, you will be taken to the full listing of Essentials playlists.

2. Browse this collection of playlists, and click on any playlists that look interesting. Read the playlist notes that accompany at least two of them.

    Note: If you only want to look at "Essentials" playlists in a certain genre then use the CHOOSE GENRE menu to go to the home page for that genre. From there, the ITUNES ESSENTIALS section will list only the playlists from that genre.

3. Buy or add to your shopping cart any songs or mixes that you feel like buying.

Day 5

1. Start up the *iTunes* jukebox player. Click on the MUSIC STORE icon in the left column. Now have a look at the CELEBRITY PLAYLISTS section, which lists music playlists put together by various performers and celebrities.

2. Browse this collection of playlists, and click on any playlists that look interesting. Read the playlist notes that accompany at least two of them. The quality of these playlists is mixed. Some of them are just blatant plugs for the performers' own music. Others have been but together with some thought, and provide interesting listening and reading.

3. Buy or add to your shopping cart any songs or mixes you feel like buying.

Day 6

1. Start up the *iTunes* jukebox player. Click on the MUSIC STORE icon in the left column. Now click on the IMIX link that appears in the left column of the music store window. This will take you to a collection of iMixes, playlists created and published by *iTunes* users, containing songs available from the iTunes Music Store.

2. Browse the available iMixes and click on a few, taking time to read any playlist notes that accompany them. The TOP RATED iMixes, based on customer feedback, are displayed. On the right side of the window, there is a SHOW IMIXES control that will let you display the MOST RECENT iMixes, regardless of rating. Look at a few of these as well. If you find an iMix that you like, click on the SEE ALL IMIXES BY THIS USER link and see if there are other iMixes created by the same person. You also have the option of rating the iMix as well.

    Note: When scanning a long iMix, it is sometimes useful to click on the ARTIST column label. This will sort the tracks alphabetically by artist.

3. To save an iMix locally for further review, use your mouse to select and drag the tracks to the left pane of your iTunes jukebox player. This will cause a new local playlist entry to appear. You will need to name it. Do this with at least one playlist. Note that you can do this with individual tracks or portions of iMix playlists as well.

4. Locate the HOW DO I CREATE AN IMIX? link and click on it. Read the brief instructions on how to publish your own iMix, should you be so inclined.

5. The other way to find iMixes is on the album and artist information pages. Use the iTunes search tool to locate an album or an artist that is well known to you. Then look for TOP RATED IMIXES that contain something from that artist or album.

6. Buy or add to your shopping cart any songs or mixes you feel like buying.

Day 7

1. Start up the *iTunes* jukebox player. Click on the MUSIC STORE icon in the left column. Now click on the BILLBOARD CHARTS link that appears in the left column of the music store window. This will open up the iTunes Music Store BROWSE window, to reveal three Billboard chart options.

2. Click on the BILLBOARD HOT 100 option. This in turn should reveal a number of YEAR options. Scroll down, look at all the options, pick a year and click on it. You will now see, in chart order, all the songs from the iTunes Music Store that were on that chart in that given year.

3. Look at the songs for that year, then look at the songs for a few other years. I recommend looking at milestone years in your life: the year you graduated from school, the year you were born, the year you were married, etc. Reading the titles of these songs will take you back in time.

4. Now return your attention to the BROWSE window. In the left pane, below the BILLBOARD CHARTS link, is a RADIO CHARTS link. Click on it. This will reveal a list of cities for which radio airplay charts are available. Click on the name of a city, perhaps your local metropolitan area. This will reveal, in the rightmost pane, a list of radio stations for which charts are available. Choose one and click on it. You will see, in chart order, all the songs from the iTunes Music Store that are on that stations airplay chart. Note that the content of the charts will reflect the format of the station (e.g., country songs for a country station).

5. Buy or add to your shopping cart any songs or albums you feel like buying.

   Note: If you are a Windows user (XP or 2000) and have decided not to continue using the *iTunes* software, make sure to uninstall it because it uses your computer's memory even when you aren't using it. Two services, *iPodService.exe* and *iTunesHelper.exe*, run in the background at all times, regardless of whether or not you are using *iTunes*.

iTunes Music Store Summary

Having completed the steps outlined you should now:

- Know the difference between the one-click purchasing method and the shopping cart purchasing method, and how to switch between them.

- Know how to browse and search for music using the *iTunes* player.

- Know how to access artist and album information.

- Be familiar with the different type of playlists available at the iTunes Music Store: the staff created iTunes Essentials playlists, the celebrity created playlists, and the listener created iMixes.

- Know how to access the different music charts available at the iTunes Music Store: the Billboard charts, the radio airplay charts, and the iTunes popularity charts.

- Know how to access Internet radio stations using the *iTunes* player.

32

eMusic Discovery Plan

What follows is a seven-day plan for getting up-to-speed with eMusic and putting its features to use. For background information on eMusic, consult Chapter 12, *eMusic: Downloading for Discovery.*

Before using the eMusic service, make sure that you have a music jukebox program that you can use to store, organize, and play MP3 music files. There are many capable, free jukebox software packages out there. Recommended packages include *Musicmatch Jukebox* for Windows users and *iTunes* for Macintosh and Windows users.

Day 1

1. Go to eMusic's Web site (http://www.emusic.com) and sign up for their free trial, which as of this writing is fourteen days long and allows fifty free downloads before you are required to subscribe. You will get a login ID and password. You will need to supply your credit card information. To avoid inadvertently activating a paying subscription, mark down the trial expiration date on your calendar and complete the steps in this plan before the expiration date.

2. Download the *eMusic Download Manager* software package when you are prompted to do so during the sign up process.

   Note: There is an option menu on the *eMusic Download Manager* software which allows you to specify which directory you want your music files downloaded to. Here you can specify whether you want separate subdirectories created for artists and/or albums when your music files are downloaded. Last, you can specify the naming convention to be used for any music files that you download. If you are unsure of what to do, you can return and do this later (default options can be used).

3. Login to the eMusic Web site (http://www.emusic.com) and scan the genre labels in the left column of the home page (e.g., ROCK/POP, JAZZ). Pick one and click on it. This will take you to the home page for that music genre.

4. Check out the albums that are highlighted on this home page. Pick one and click on the title. This will load the album information page for that album. Find the LISTEN TO ALL link, just below the listing of tracks, and click on it. This will load thirty-second samples of all the tracks into your music player. As the track samples play, read the album review (if one is available). Then scan the list of RELATED ARTISTS.

5. If you decide you want the album, click on the DOWNLOAD ALL link which—after a moment—will launch the *eMusic Download Manager* software and begin the download process. If you're not sure, but would like to keep track of the album, then click on the SAVE FOR LATER link, which will place the album into your SAVE FOR LATER list.

   Note: To conserve your quota of available downloads you can choose to download a few songs from an album rather than the whole thing. Above the DOWNLOAD ALL link are check marks next to each song; clicking on one will download just that track. You can always go back and download the rest of the tracks later.

6. Go back to the genre home page and browse some more. Take some time to read the featured article written by one of eMusic's columnists. If you haven't already downloaded an album or some tracks, find some and download them.

7. Play your downloaded music using your jukebox software.

   Note: If you have problems using the service, go to the eMusic help page where you can access support information and contact their support staff if necessary. The HELP link is available on every page in the upper right hand corner. If you are having a problem with your jukebox software, use the help files and support options provided by the manufacturer.

Day 2

1. Now it's time to check eMusic for albums by artists that you recognize. Login to the eMusic Web site (http://www.emusic.com) and click on the BROWSE button on the toolbar at the top of the page. This will load the top-level BROWSE page on eMusic.

2. Now turn your attention to the left column. Down near the bottom you will find a VIEW ALL (A TO Z) heading. Click on the link beneath it which reads ARTISTS. This will load an enormous alphabetical listing of artists (over 24,000, as I write this). Now turn your attention to the links in the left column, under the heading which reads REFINE BY. Clicking on these links will narrow the list down.

3. Click on the link which reads TOP ALBUMS. Note that the list of artists has now gotten considerably smaller. Now click on the link with reads EDITOR'S PICKS. Note that the list has gotten smaller still. What you are seeing is a list of all artists whose albums are both popular on eMusic *and* acclaimed by eMusic editors. Now you have two choices: browse through this list of artists, which is still quite large, or, click on another REFINE BY link to trim the list down further. You have the option of refining the list by genre and then style, by decade, or even by featured region.

    Spend at least thirty minutes scanning these artist lists. Click on the names of artists that interest you. This will take you to artist information pages, where you can read brief biographies and see the albums they have available on eMusic. Clicking on the album names will take you to album pages where you can read a review, play music samples, download tracks, or save the album to your SAVE FOR LATER list.

4. Find an album to download, then download and play it using your jukebox software.

Optional

*   Share your opinion of the album with other eMusic subscribers. Use the RATE IT or WRITE A REVIEW links on the album information page to rate the album and/or write a review.

Day 3

1. Now is the time to look for interesting music by artists you never heard of! Login to the eMusic Web site (http://www.emusic.com) and scan the genre labels in the left column of the home page (e.g., ROCK/POP, JAZZ). Pick one that you are *unfamiliar* with and click on it. This will take you to the home page for that genre category.

2. Read the featured column for that genre. In it you'll find references to music available on eMusic, with links to album, artist, and record label pages. If you see albums that interest you, bookmark them with the SAVE FOR LATER link.

3. Go back to the genre home page and turn your attention to the STYLE links in the left column. Pick a style and click on it. This will open up a list of all the albums in that style, probably a big list. Click on EDITOR'S PICKS link in the left column to narrow the list down further. If the list is still too big, refine it by clicking on another REFINE BY link (decade, region, or recent additions). Now browse the albums and artists listed, and save any interesting albums to your SAVE FOR LATER list.

3. Repeat this process for at least one more style within the genre you selected.

4. Now take a look at your SAVE FOR LATER list. Go to the QUICK LINKS pull-down menu in the upper left corner of the page, open it up, and then scroll down and select the entry that reads SAVED FOR LATER. Pick one entry from your list and then download it and play it. If you have trouble deciding, read reviews and use the LISTEN TO ALL link to play track samples. If you don't have any albums in your SAVE FOR LATER list, then you need to browse some more. Get going!

Day 4

1. Go to the eMusic Web site (http://www.emusic.com) and login. Now click on the MESSAGE BOARDS link—located among the links at the bottom of the page (as of this writing). The message boards are a good place to learn about interesting albums.

2. Once you have entered the message boards area, you will see links to genre specific message boards, as well as a listing of the most recent postings across all the message boards. After briefly scanning this list of postings, choose a genre specific message board and click on the link for it. Browse the postings and look for album recommendations.

3. When you find an album recommendation of interest, use the eMusic search tool to find the album page, where you can read a review (if available) and use the LISTEN TO ALL link to sample all the tracks on the album. Use the SAVE FOR LATER link to bookmark promising albums.

4. Download and play one album.

Optional

- Use the message boards to post questions or start discussions with other eMusic subscribers. For more information on using online message boards see chapter 25, *Finding People Who Share Your Interests*.

Day 5

You should now be close to using up the free downloads that came with your trial subscription. It's time to decide whether an active subscription would be worth it. There are three monthly plans available:

	Tracks	Monthly Fee	Per Track Cost
eMusic Basic	40	$9.99	$0.25
eMusic Plus	60	$14.99	$0.23
eMusic Premium	90	$19.99	$0.22

The eMusic Basic plan buys you roughly three albums worth of music for ten dollars while the eMusic Premium plan buys you roughly five albums of music for fifteen dollars. One drawback to these plans is that unused tracks will not carry over to the next month. This means your actual cost per track will be higher unless you are diligent about using up your 40 allocated tracks each month. Additional tracks, that *do* carry over, can be purchased in the form of "booster packs." A 10 track booster pack costs $4.99 (50 cents per track); a 25 track pack costs $9.99 (40 cents per track); a 50 track pack costs $14.99 (30 cents per track).

Use the ACCOUNT link at the top right of the page to access your account page, where you can cancel or upgrade your subscription, buy booster packs, or change your payment information. The account page is also where you can sign up for genre-specific newsletters, delivered by e-mail, that will alert you to new albums available on eMusic.

If you decide to activate a paying subscription, then find another album or at least a few more songs to download and play. If not, you still have the option of finishing out this eMusic Discovery Plan; you just won't be able to download any more music once your 50 free tracks are used up.

Day 6

1. Go to the eMusic Web site (http://www.emusic.com) and login. Now click on the YOUR PROFILE button on the toolbar at the top of the page. This will load a page from which you can manage your personal information on eMusic.

2. Click on the EDIT PROFILE button. This will load a form in which you can supply personal information (optionally) for other members of the eMusic community to see. Fill out the form as much or as little as you like and SUBMIT any changes.

3. Click on the DOWNLOADS button. This will load a list of all the tracks you have downloaded from eMusic, tracks that you can download again without incurring charges against your monthly quota of tracks.

4. Click on the LISTS button. This will load your music lists page, where you can create lists of favorite albums and tracks with commentary, lists that you can make public or keep private. Any lists that you have already created will be accessible here.

5. Take note of the RATINGS and REVIEWS buttons. Click on these to see any album ratings or reviews that you have entered into the system.

6. Now click on the NEIGHBORS button. This will load a list of eMusic sub-scribers whose downloading patterns are similar to yours. They may be anonymous members, in which case they'll be assigned a number (e.g., *EMUSIC-00549CF5*). Otherwise, they'll be listed by their chosen eMusic nickname. Click on one of your NEIGHBORS to see their profile. Then browse their eMusic DOWNLOADS collection, and their RATINGS, REVIEWS, and LISTS (if they have any).

   If you like their profile, you can click on the ADD AS A FRIEND link to make your "neighbor" into a "friend"; they will then be listed whenever you click the FRIENDS button. While your NEIGHBORS list can change, your FRIENDS list will not; unless, of course, you change it yourself.

   Note: Many of these features were rolled-out just as this book was going to press. So the amount of community-created content (ratings, reviews, etc.) is still small. The message boards and subscriber-created favorite music lists are an exception, because they have been around for a while.

Day 7

1. Login to the eMusic Web site (http://www.emusic.com) and click on the CHARTS button on the toolbar at the top of the page. If you haven't already, take a look at the available charts and sample some of the popular albums and tracks. Also take a look at the TOP LABELS listing. Click on a couple of the links and read about the record labels.

2. Now click on the EMUSIC LIVE button on the toolbar at the top of the page, which will take you to the eMusic Live home page. Read the brief description of the eMusic Live program, and then click on the link below, in small text, which reads VIEW ALL EMUSIC LIVE VENUES. This will take you to a page describing the eMusic Live program in greater detail. Read this page, then go back to the eMusic Live home page and browse the offerings. Sample some of the music.

3. Find an album to download, anywhere on the eMusic Web site, then download and play it using your jukebox software.

4. You should have some time left on your trial subscription. If you don't intend to use the service anymore, cancel now to avoid paying a monthly fee. If you do intend to continue with eMusic, enjoy! (your subscription will convert automatically). Many happy discoveries are ahead.

eMusic Summary

Having completed the steps outlined you should now:

- Have successfully downloaded and played tracks from eMusic.

- Have used eMusic supplied reviews, artist information, and music columns to identify new and interesting albums.

- Know how to use the BROWSE pages and REFINE BY links to effectively navigate eMusic's catalog.

- Have used the message boards to discover albums of interest.

- Know what the subscription options are and how to sign up for genre specific eMusic newsletters.

- Know how to use the SAVE FOR LATER list and YOUR PROFILE page.

- Have a bigger library of music available to use for CD-burning or local playback.

33

Musicmatch Online Discovery Plan

What follows is a seven-day plan for getting up-to-speed with Musicmatch Online. For background on Musicmatch's online services, consult Chapter 13, *Musicmatch Online: One-Stop Shop for Digital Music.*

Day 1

1. Go to the Musicmatch Web site (http://www.musicmatch.com) and follow the instructions for downloading and installing the *Musicmatch Jukebox* software. You will be given a choice between the "Basic", free player and the "Plus" player, which they charge a fee for. Choose the Basic player. If you decide later you want the extra features in the "Plus" version, you can always upgrade.

   Note: These instructions are based on version 9.0 of the *Musicmatch Jukebox* software. They also assume that you are using the default interface or "skin" that comes with version 9.0.

2. During installation you will be given a choice of whether or not you want to PERSONALIZE MUSIC AND RECOMMENDATIONS. If you reply YES, you are authorizing Musicmatch to upload information on the songs you play using *Musicmatch Jukebox*. This lets them provide you personalized music recommendations. If you have privacy concerns, then decline this option. This feature can be turned on later if you desire.

3. Sign up for a free trial of the Musicmatch On-Demand service. This will give you access to all of Musicmatch's subscription services. As of this writing, Musicmatch is offering a seven-day free trial of the on-demand service, which requires that you supply them with credit card information. You will then get a login ID and password. To avoid inadvertently activating a paying subscription, mark down the trial expiration date on your calendar and complete the steps in this plan before the expiration date. Here, you also have the option of enabling *Musicmatch Downloads*, a service which allows you to purchase portable downloads. Enabling this option won't cost you anything.

4. Start up the *Musicmatch Jukebox* player software either by clicking on the desktop icon that was installed during installation or by using the entry for it on the Windows PROGRAMS menu. Click on the RADIO button on the left hand column of the player. Then click on the LOGIN button and login using your ID and password. If you check the REMEMBER ME box, you will be automatically logged in the next time you access the service—assuming you are using the same computer.

   Note: I have found that Musicmatch doesn't always "remember me." So I recommend keeping your ID and password handy.

5. Review the STATIONS menu on the left hand side of the Radio window. Browse the category listing and click on a category that interests you. This will open up a list of stations in that category. Click on the name of a station that interests you. This will take you to a station information page. Here, click on the PLAY THIS STATION button. Listen for at least fifteen minutes. If you don't like a song, use the skip button to move to the next track. Check out other stations if you're interested.

   Note: Holding down the ALT key while hitting the right-arrow key will also let you skip to the next song.

6. If you like the radio station you are listening to, click on the FAVORITES button on the right side of the screen and select the ADD TO FAVORITES option. This will place a link to this station in this favorites folder, visible whenever you click on the FAVORITES button. To delete a station from this list, click on the EDIT FAVORITES link, also on this menu. This will take you to a FAVORITES MANAGER page where you can click on the X button to delete the station.

7. If necessary, adjust the quality of the music stream you are receiving by clicking on the CD QUALITY button next to the label. This will toggle the setting back and forth between LOW and CD. If you have a broadband connection select CD. If you have a low speed or less reliable connection, pick LOW to prevent interruptions. It may take a song or two for the new setting to take effect.

8. While you are listening, click the NOW PLAYING button on the left hand side of the player. This will load information about the current album in the main window. See if there is a review of the album available. If there is, read it. Then click on the artist's name, where it is underlined, to load the artist information page. Now click on the ARTIST INFO tab on the right side of the page. Explore the types of information offered. As of this writing, this includes the following sections for each artist: BIOGRAPHY, DISCOGRAPHY, ROOTS AND INFLUENCES, and ARTIST IN-DEPTH. Also review the RELATED ARTISTS links, just above, to see related artists that other

Musicmatch users are listening to. Clicking on these links will take you the artist pages for these artists.

Note: Another easy way to access artist and album information is to place your cursor over a song on the playlist and right-clicking with your mouse. This will reveal a menu with the options: GO TO ARTIST PAGE and GO TO ALBUM PAGE. Clicking on one of these selections takes you to the page in question. This method also has the advantage of letting you look up information about tracks that aren't currently playing.

9. If you hear a song that intrigues you—perhaps you've never heard the artist before—and want to keep track of it, use the MY WISHLIST feature. Go to the playlist display and place your cursor over the track you are interested in. Right click with your mouse. When the menu of options appears, click on selection that reads ADD TRACK(S) TO MY WISHLIST. Try adding one song. This way you can return later to research the song, play it, or buy it. This is available from the same right click menu discussed in the last step. One of the other options is VIEW MY WISHLIST. Select that option when you want to view or edit your wishlist.

Note: Your Musicmatch Wishlist lets you bookmark any track that plays on Musicmatch Radio. For licensing reasons some of these tracks are not available for downloading or on-demand playback. If such a track is available for downloading, you'll see the a BUY TRACK button next to it on the playlist display window. If not, you'll see an ARTIST INFO button next to the track instead. In most cases, if a track is available for downloading, it is also available for on-demand playback.

Phew! That's enough for one day.

Day 2

1. Start up *Musicmatch Jukebox* and login if necessary. Click on the RADIO button. Now click on the JUMP TO button, located on the top left hand side of the radio information window. A pull-down menu will appear. Place your cursor over the STATIONS option—another menu will appear—and then move your cursor over the LAST PLAYED option and click. This will launch the last radio station you were listening to.

2. Listen for a few minutes until you find a track that interests you. If you like, you can use the skip button to speed this process up. Place your cursor over the track and right-click to open a menu. Click on the selection that reads GO TO ARTIST PAGE. This should load the artist page in the main window.

3. As you look at this page, take note of whether you see play buttons for either an ARTIST MATCH station, an ARTIST RADIO station, or both. These would appear right under the artist's name. Depending on the licensing arrangements that Musicmatch has with that artist's record label(s), you will see one, both, or neither. For the purpose of this exercise, I would like you to find an artist page that has both ARTIST MATCH and ARTIST RADIO stations available. So if need be, repeat step two until you find one. This will work better if you are truly interested in the artist in question.

4. Click the ARTIST RADIO station PLAY button and listen for a least fifteen minutes. Add this station to your Favorites list by clicking on the FAVOR-ITES button and then the ADD TO FAVORITES selection.

5. Click on the NOW PLAYING button to access the album information pages for the tracks being played. If reviews are available, read them.

6. If you haven't discovered this already, try double clicking on the album cover image located on the upper left side of the player. This will open up a separate window with a larger version of the image. I have found that I can use my mouse to resize this window—I like making it bigger—and that the new size takes effect the next time I double click on an album cover image.

7. Now go back to the artist page and click the ARTIST MATCH station PLAY button and listen for a least fifteen minutes. If a track doesn't appeal to you, use the skip button to move forward. Take note of how this station differs from the ARTIST RADIO station for the same artist. Remember also to add any interesting tracks to your Wishlist for future reference.

Day 3

1. Start up *Musicmatch Jukebox* and login if necessary. Review the genre categories on the stations menu, clicking on them to reveal the stations in each category. Take note that most of the genre category folders have an ALL [GENRE] STYLES link in them (e.g., ALL BLUES STYLES).

2. Click on the ALL [GENRE] STYLES link in a few major genre categories and review the available options. Note that some of these options are not visible on the main category menu. When you find a music style of interest, click on it. A station information page will appear. Now click on the PLAY THIS STATION button and read the GENRE INFO that is provided. Listen to this station for at least fifteen minutes. Add it to your Favorites.

3. Once the station has started to play, click on the NOW PLAYING button and read the album reviews associated with the tracks that are played. Wait until you come across a track that really interests you. If need be, use the skip button to speed this process up.

    If tracks from this album are available for purchase, the screen will tell you so. This is because you are in the MUSIC STORE VIEW for the album. With your active on-demand trial subscription, however, you have the option of playing the album without buying it (assuming it's available for on-demand streaming). In order to do so, you will need to switch to the ON DEMAND VIEW for this album.

4. Place your cursor somewhere in the album information window and right-click with your mouse. A small menu will open up. Click on the option that reads ON DEMAND VIEW. This will load the ON DEMAND VIEW for this album. If the album is available for on-demand streaming you have two options: PLAY ALBUM and SAVE TO LIBRARY. First, click on the SAVE TO LIBRARY button. This will allow you to retrieve the album later from your *Musicmatch Jukebox* library. Now click the PLAY ALBUM button and listen to the album. If the album is not available for on-demand streaming, continue to listen to the radio station and reading album reviews until you find an interesting album that you can play.

5. If you haven't already, try switching to the compact, MINI VIEW of *Musicmatch Jukebox*. There is a small icon with a downward pointing arrow to the left of the standard MINIMIZE and MAXIMIZE icons at the top right of the Musicmatch window. Click on this to switch to the MINI VIEW. Clicking on the same icon, which is now pointing upward, will reverse this process. Another way to switch to MINI VIEW is to simultaneously type the ALT and PAGE DOWN keys on your keyboard. The reverse is accomplished by simultaneously typing the ALT and PAGE UP keys.

Day 4

1. Think of a period in your life, between 1960 and the present, that you would like to revisit musically. It could be the year you were born, your senior year in high school, or the year you got married. Alternately, you can pick a year or decade that interests you musically.

2. Start up *Musicmatch Jukebox* and login if necessary. Click on the RADIO button. Now browse the ERA menu, just below the STATIONS menu. You'll find a folder for each decade. Open a folder and click on a year or decade that interests you. This will load the station information page.

3. Click on the PLAY THIS STATION button and listen for at least ten minutes, skipping tracks whenever necessary. Click on the FAVORITES button and then click to ADD TO FAVORITES. While you are listening to this station, click on the TRACKS FROM THIS ERA tab and take a look at the tracks listed. Remember also to add any interesting tracks to your Wishlist for future reference.

4. Now switch to the ON DEMAND VIEW by placing your cursor somewhere in the station information window and right-clicking with your mouse and selecting the ON DEMAND VIEW option. Now you can pick and choose from the TRACKS FROM THIS ERA list. Scan the list, and choose five tracks. Click on the PLAY button next to each of these tracks. This will load the tracks into your playlist window and start playing them. Note that you can reorder the playlist by using your mouse to drag tracks up or down in the playlist.

5. Click the SAVE button, located just below the playlist display. A SAVE PLAYLIST dialog box will open up and prompt you to give the playlist a name. Name the playlist and click on the OK button. To reload that playlist in the future, simply click on the PLAYLIST button and select it from the list that is displayed.

Optional

- While you are listening, pick a song or album that you'd like to buy and make portable. Then download it and play it. Your credit card will be charged accordingly. This will introduce you to the *Musicmatch Downloads* service.

Day 5

1. Today you're going to create a music mix using Musicmatch On-Demand. Think of an idea for a music mix playlist. It could be as simple as a collection of your favorite songs. Or you could be more ambitious and create a playlist based on a theme, a setting, or an occasion. If you need ideas, take a look at the Art of the Mix Web site: http://www.artofthemix.org.

2. Start up the *Musicmatch Jukebox* player software and login if necessary. Click on the ON DEMAND button, which will load the ON DEMAND service home page.

3. Use the search tool to find songs for your playlist, searching by TRACK or, if necessary, by ARTIST or ALBUM. When you search by TRACK, you'll often find (for popular songs) that there are multiple versions, on different albums, performed by different artists. In these cases, clicking the ARTIST column heading will sort the listing by artist, which can be helpful. Some tracks will be available for on-demand playback; others will not.

4. As you find songs that are playable, click on the PLAY button to load the song into your playlist window. It will start to play. Continue to add songs until you have at least five or six (you can always return later to add more). To reorder tracks, use your mouse to drag tracks up or down in the playlist.

5. Click the SAVE button, located just below the playlist display. A SAVE PLAYLIST dialog box will open up and prompt you to give the playlist a name. Name the playlist and click on the OK button. To reload that playlist in the future, simply click on the PLAYLIST button and select it from the list that is displayed.

6. Now click on the SEND TO button, which is also located below the playlist display. A small pull down menu will appear. Select the option that reads A FRIEND (E-MAIL TRACK LIST). This will open up the SEND TO A FRIEND window. Fill out the form and send the playlist to yourself via e-mail, taking note of the text which explains what both subscribers and nonsubscribers can do with these playlists. If you have friends or family members you'd like to send the playlist to, add their e-mail addresses to the "send to" list. Then click the SEND PLAYLIST button. Later, check your e-mail and see what the playlist mailing looks like.

Day 6

1. Today you'll be revisiting your Musicmatch Wishlist. Start up the *Music-match Jukebox* player software and login if necessary. Click on the RADIO button. Pick a radio station and start playing it.

2. Now click on the small TOOLS button that appears to the right side of the player, just below the search box. A small pull-down menu will appear. Click on the option that reads VIEW WISHLIST. By now you should have a few tracks on your Wishlist. If you don't have any, take the time to add a few tracks from the station you are now listening to (for the sake of demonstration). To do this, place your cursor over a track, right-click with your mouse, and then select the ADD TRACKS TO MY WISHLIST option.

3. Review the items on your Wishlist. Pick one item from the list and click on the album name; this will take you to the album page. Click on the ALBUM INFO tab and read the review, if there is one. Now, let's see if the album is available for on-demand playback. While your cursor is still inside the album information window, right-click with your mouse and select the ON DEMAND VIEW option. The album information page will now be in the ON DEMAND VIEW. Play the album if you are able. If you end up liking the album, click on the SAVE TO LIBRARY button to save it to your Musicmatch Library.

4. While you are listening to the album (or radio station if the album isn't available), take the time to check out Musicmatch's keyboard shortcuts. Take a look at the *Musicmatch Jukebox* Help pages. There is an entry for SHORTCUT KEYS. Here you will find a number of functions that can be executed quickly from the keyboard. These shortcuts can make your use of *Musicmatch Jukebox* more efficient. Try some out.

Day 7

1. Start up the *Musicmatch Jukebox* player software and login if necessary. Click on the RADIO button.

2. Click on the FAVORITES button and then click on one of the radio stations which appears on this list. Begin listening. Now click on the FAVORITES button again, but this time click on the EDIT FAVORITES option. Review the stations you have saved thus far and delete any that you no longer want on the list.

3. With your free trial about to expire, you need to cancel the subscription or choose one of their plans: Musicmatch Gold, Musicmatch Platinum, or Musicmatch On-Demand. If you choose one of these plans you will also need to pick a billing period: monthly, quarterly, and yearly. The longer the billing period and thus commitment, the lower your monthly rate will be. If you choose a longer billing period, you will be charged up-front for the entire period.

   If you make no choice, the plan will automatically be converted to an On-Demand subscription and your credit card will be charged the annual fee. If you need to try some other services—or just need more time before deciding—then cancel now. You can sign up for a paying subscription once you've made your decision. In the meantime, you can use the free Musicmatch Radio service.

Musicmatch Online Summary

Having completed the steps outlined you should now:

- Be familiar with the selection of radio stations available to Musicmatch Radio users, including the GENRE, ERA, and ARTIST stations.

- Be able to play ARTIST MATCH and ARTIST RADIO stations and know the difference between them.

- Be able to use the *Musicmatch Jukebox* player controls, including the MY WISHLIST and FAVORITES features.

- Understand how to use the Musicmatch On-Demand service , including how to create and share on-demand (streaming) playlists via e-mail.

- Be able to retrieve artist, album, and music genre information pages using *Musicmatch Jukebox.*

- Be able to switch between the MUSIC STORE VIEW, the ON DEMAND VIEW, and the RADIO VIEW when looking at music information pages.

- Understand how to use Musicmatch Downloads to purchase music.

Glossary

AAC (Advanced Audio Coding)
A recently developed audio file format developed by the Moving Picture Experts Group (MPEG), the same group that produced the MP3 format. For more information see: http://www.aac-audio.com. AAC is used by Apple for its iTunes Music Store downloads, in conjunction with an Apple proprietary *DRM* scheme called Fairplay.

Arbitron
A company that measures radio usage and produces lists of the most popular Internet radio stations and networks. URL: http://www.arbitron.com.

Artist Radio
Feature offered with MusicMatch's Platinum radio service, formerly called "Artist On-Demand." Artist Radio lets you play contiguous blocks of music by a given artist. It does not, however, let you choose which specific songs get played, or the order in which they get played. As such, it is a *near on-demand* service which, for less money, provides an alternative to *online jukebox* services.

ASCAP (American Society of Composers, Authors and Publishers)
U.S. based association that licenses public performances of copyrighted works and collects and distributed royalties for these performances.

Audio File Format
Audio file formats specify how sound information is stored in digital files. File formats can differ in a number ways, including how they store audio information, whether they compress that information, and what software and hardware can be used with them. Popular audio file formats include *MP3* and WMA (Windows Media Player audio format).

Audio Player
Software that lets you play audio files on your computer—also referred to as a media player. Popular audio players include *Musicmatch Jukebox, Winamp, RealPlayer, Windows Media Player*, and *iTunes*. Some of these players handle video as well.

Bandwidth
The capacity of an Internet connection as measured in kilobits per second (thousands) or megabits per second (millions).

Bit Rate

The amount of data that your Internet connection can deliver, measured in kilobits (thousands of bits) or megabits (millions of bits) per second. Bit rate can also refer to the quality of a digitally encoded sound recording. A recording encoded at a bit rate of 128 kilobits per second (Kbps) will contain twice the information, and thus better sound quality, than a recording encoded at a bit rate of 64 kilobits per second (Kbps). To receive streaming music, your Internet connection must have a bit rate that equals or exceeds the bit rate of the files being delivered.

BMI (Broadcast Music, Inc.)

Like *ASCAP*, BMI is a U.S.-based performing rights organization that licenses public performances of copyrighted works and collects and distributes royalties for these performances.

Bricks and mortar retailers

Stores with physical locations that you can visit.

Broadband

Internet connections capable of rapid data transfer. *Cable* and *DSL* connections are regarded as "broadband" connections whereas low-speed dial-up connections are not.

Buffering

When a streaming music file is delivered to an audio player, the player needs to have a certain amount of that file available in a local buffer (or storage area) in order for the music to play. Buffering is the process of ensuring that this requirement is met. Frequent buffering messages and music interruptions occur when your Internet connection can't deliver the music file fast enough to keep up with your player.

Burn

To create a music CD by copying digital music files to a blank CD. This requires a writable CD-ROM drive. See also: *Rip*.

Cable Internet Access

Internet connections using a cable modem and a coaxial cable, often using the same line used to provide Cable TV service. Like DSL, cable access is a high-speed or *broadband* connection.

CARP (Copyright Arbitration Royalty Panel)

Ad-hoc panels appointed by the Librarian of Congress to make recommendations concerning issues that arise concerning copyright royalty payments and distributions. Recent CARP recommendations dealing with royalties owed by Internet radio broadcasters were the focus of much attention and controversy. More information is available at: http://www.copyright.gov/carp.

CDDB Music Recognition Service

An Internet-based service used by numerous media players to identify music files being played and display track and album information in the player. This widely used database contains more than 1.8 million CDs and 20 million songs and is owned by the company Gracenote. For more information see: http://www.gracenote.com/gn_products/cddb.html.

CD Quality / "Near CD quality"

CD quality refers to the audio quality of music CDs you buy in the store. Technically, this means that music is digitally sampled at a rate of 44,100 samples per second with a bit depth of 16 bits (each sample contains 16 bits of information) in two separate channels. Most Internet-delivered music is not of CD quality. Improving *codecs*, though, promise to change this. "Near CD quality" is a term used by Internet music services to denote higher quality audio streams that fall short of CD quality.

Codec

Codec is short for "Coder/Decoder." An audio codec is software that compresses and encodes audio data into a particular *audio file format*. Improving codecs have made it possible to deliver higher quality sound using smaller files and lower bandwidth Internet connections.

Collaborative Filtering

The process of analyzing the preferences or actions of a group of people and using them to supply individuals with personalized recommendations (e.g., people who bought this CD also bought these CDs).

Digital Millennium Copyright Act (DMCA)

Controversial revision (1998) of U.S. copyright law which addressed issues raised by digital technology. These included "fair use" of copyrighted materials in the digital environment, circumvention of copyright protection systems, and Internet service provider liability for copyright violations.

Downloads

Files that are copied to your computer and available for local use and playback, regardless of whether or not you are connected to the Internet. See also *tethered downloads*.

Downloading Services

Services that allow you to download music files to store on your computer. See also *tethered downloads*.

DRM (Digital Rights Management)

The process and technologies used by content owners to control who gets access to their digital content and what can be done with that content. Major label download stores use DRM to restrict what you can do with the music.

DSL (Digital Subscriber Line)
DSL is a technology for bringing high-bandwidth connectivity to homes and small businesses over existing telephone lines. DSL is considered a form of *broadband.*

Fair Use
Fair use refers to situations where limited copying or distribution of published works without the author's permission is allowed under copyright law. Examples include the use of excerpts for critique or review and limited use by teachers for educational purposes.

File Trading Services
Controversial services that facilitate the sharing of music files over the Internet (often in violation of copyright law), including the original incarnation of *Napster* and its successors, *Kazaa*, eDonkey, Morpheus, and others.

Filtering
When network administrators restrict user access to certain Internet resources, including Web sites. This happens in the workplace and in certain schools and libraries as well.

Firewall
Security software used to regulate computer traffic going in and out of a private network—such as in a company, school, or home—and protect network resources from unauthorized uses. Firewalls can present a barrier to music streaming if they are not configured appropriately.

Harry Fox Agency (HFA)
On behalf of music publishers, HFA issues licenses and collects and distributes royalties for the mechanical reproduction of copyrighted recordings. This is in contrast to agencies such as *ASCAP* and *BMI*, which license the performance rights to copyrighted recordings.

Indies
Independent record labels.

Invisible Web
That portion of the Web that is not visible to major search engines like Google, which are limited in the types of content they can index. This includes content stored in databases that are accessible only via a specific search interface.

ISDN (Integrated Services Digital Network)
Another type of broadband connection available to Internet users. Eclipsed in popularity by cable modem and *DSL* connections, ISDN is an older technology that is the only broadband option in some areas.

Internet Radio Service
A collection of radio stations offered through a single organization and accessible from a single dedicated player interface.

Internet Service Providers (ISPs)
Companies that sell Internet access to consumers and businesses.

Kazaa
Once the most popular peer-to-peer (P2P) file-trading service, Kazaa is currently being eclipsed by a newer service, eDonkey.

Listmania
Feature on Amazon.com that lets customers create annotated lists of any product sold on their site (e.g. books, CDs). Customers are free to create themes or topics for their lists (e.g., my favorite blues records).

Major Labels
Otherwise known as the "Big 5," these companies dominate the recorded music industry. They are BMG Entertainment, EMI Group, Sony Music Entertainment, Warner Brothers, and Universal Music Group.

Metadata
Data that describes an information object (e.g., book, CD, music file). In the case of a music file, this would include information such as song title, album name, genre of music, and date published.

MP3
MP3 is a popular *audio file format* used to store music files on computers. Its use of compression techniques to shrink the size of music files played a big role in the evolution of digital music on the Internet. MP3 stands for Motion Picture Experts Group, Audio Layer 3.

MP3PRO
A newer version of the MP3 format that uses improved file compression techniques to store an equivalent music file in half the space that would be required for an MP3 file.

Napster
The original peer-to-peer (P2P) file trading service, created by college student Shawn Fanning and responsible for introducing millions to file trading. Napster was shutdown in 2001 as the result of legal action by the music industry. The name and trademark are currently owned by Roxio Inc., which released a Napster-branded online music service in October 2003. This service is discussed in Chapter 14, *Napster and other On-Demand Services.*

Near On-Demand
Refers to personalized Internet radio services that allow you to control the overall content of a playlist by specifying the music you want to hear. They fall short of providing full playlist control in that you cannot control the exact composition and sequence of the playlist.

Netiquette
Etiquette for Internet users. This most often refers to appropriate behavior when using e-mail or participating in online communities. To find Web sites with information about Netiquette, consult the Google directory entry at: http://directory.google.com/Top/Computers/Internet/Etiquette.

On-Demand Service
Service which lets you play or download any songs or albums you wish, in whatever order you wish. These include online jukebox and downloading services.

Online Jukebox
An on-demand music service that works like a jukebox: select the songs you want to play and they will be streamed via the Internet to your computer and stereo. They are sometimes called "streaming services." In order to play songs with an online jukebox you have to be connected to the Internet. This is in contrast to a downloading service, which allows you to download the music files to your own computer for offline use. Many music services combine an online jukebox service with a downloading service.

P2P (Peer to Peer)
A networking technology that allows individual computer users to share resources with one another. P2P technology is at the heart of file-trading services like *Kazaa* and Morpheus, and before that *Napster*.

RIAA (Recording Industry Association of America)
The trade group and lobbying arm of the U.S. record industry best known for its aggressive tactics in fighting music piracy. RIAA also issues gold and platinum album awards to recognize high-selling albums.

Rip / Ripper
To "rip" a CD is to copy the audio tracks from a CD onto a computer's hard drive. A Ripper is a piece of software that does this.

SESAC (The Society of European Stage Authors and Composers)
SESAC is the third major performing rights organization, along with ASCAP and BMI, which licenses public performances of copyrighted works and collects and distributes royalties for these performances.

Skins
Some audio player software gives you the option of customizing the look and feel of the player. By selecting a "skin" you can give your audio player a very specific look or personality.

Spam
Unsolicited commercial, "junk" e-mail that clogs e-mail inboxes, a serious problem on the Internet.

Spyware
Software loaded on your computer—often without your knowing about it—that "phones home" to its maker and reports on your Web surfing activities. Spyware gets loaded when you use some of the file trading applications, such as Kazaa.

Stream
A stream is an audio or video file that is delivered to your computer over the Internet and played as it is received. To play a stream you must be connected to the Internet. A *download*, by contrast, is a file that gets stored locally on your computer. Downloads are available for playback regardless of whether or not you are connected to the Internet.

Tethered Downloads
Downloaded files whose usage is restricted by Digital Rights Management (DRM) technology. For example, a music file could be played only on the computer to which it was downloaded. Or the file may "expire" after a certain date, or require an active subscription for it to be usable.

WMA (Windows Media Audio)
An audio file format developed by Microsoft and used by a number of major label download stores to deliver *DRM*-protected music.

Index

W

Printed in the United States
27661LVS00001B/105-106

9 781932 340020